IN SEARCH OF LOST CITIES

Is there a child ever born who is not curious? So, to capture their imagination, Sreelata Menon hopes to not only introduce them to the rich cultural and historical heritage of our inherited past, but also to inspire and tickle their fancy with magical stories from ancient and famous mythologies.

With more than a dozen books for children to her credit, **Sreelata Menon**, an unashamed history buff, writes on anything and everything, and can be reached at sreelata0@yahoo.co.in.

Other books by the author:

Epicurious: The Greatest Epics and Classics from India and around the World

The Fearless Twins and Other Sibling Stories from Mythology

The Invincible Heroes and Other Friendship Stories from Mythology

501 Facts Factory-Amazing Buildings of the World

IN SEARCH OF LOST CITIES

In India and around the World

Sreelata Menon

hachette
INDIA

First published in paperback in 2025 by Hachette India
(Registered name: Hachette Book Publishing India Pvt. Ltd)
An Hachette UK company
www.hachetteindia.com

1

ISBN 978-93-5731-874-7

Hachette Book Publishing India Pvt. Ltd
4th & 5th Floors, Corporate Centre
Plot No. 94, Sector 44, Gurugram – 122003, India

Typeset by Manmohan Kumar, Delhi

Printed and bound in India
by Manipal Technologies Limited

MIX
Paper | Supporting responsible forestry
FSC™ C043100
FSC
www.fsc.org

CONTENTS

OCEANIA

SO, WHAT ON EARTH ARE 'LOST CITIES'?

'Arriving at each new city, the traveller finds again a past of his that he did not know he had.' – Italo Calvino

Imagine you are walking across a large open field, perhaps near a riverbank.

Suddenly, you chance upon some peculiar mounds of grit, stone and dust.

Some large, some small.

Your curiosity aroused, you walk around it. You try to climb over it.

You kick at the rubble.

The earth loosens and out tumble some curious, mud-encrusted artefacts, perhaps some battered coins as well.

And, if you happened to be a student of archaeology or historical research, what would you do?

Your heart pounding in breathless anticipation, you would call in the experts.

These experts would then carefully dig around the mound.

More random items and perhaps the top of a brick wall or two may stick out.

They would study them minutely and when they are done, they would nod excitedly.

You would then leap into the air, pumping your fists exultantly – yess!

And, hey presto, you would have the remains of a forgotten and mysterious lost city on your hands.

'Lost' city?

Really?

A button, a shoe or maybe even a car could get lost.

Could entire populated cities get lost… or even found thus?

Well, you love solving puzzles, don't you?

Lost-and-found cities are like gigantic jigsaw puzzles.

So, if you were that student of archaeology, gazing at the random items, the artefacts that have been dug up, you would first wonder what the curious objects could be.

Next you would begin to wonder, who they belonged to – to which city and to which era in history – and how they ended up buried and lost in the mud under the mound?

And then, just like a detective solving a mystery, you would start to piece them together.

You would carefully excavate and go even deeper around the site.

You may find a few more objects in shards and fragments, and maybe one that is merely cracked and not completely broken.

It looks like a goblet, it feels like a goblet, so a goblet it has to be.

Wouldn't you be over the moon with excitement if the goblet turned out to be something that once belonged to a city – say, in Egypt – dating back to the ancient period when the famous Pharoah Tutankhamun reigned? Or even more thrilled to discover you were holding a cup that might have been used by the Mughal emperor Shah Jahan, or perhaps Emperor Ashoka, or even Lord Buddha – from a time you have only ever read about in books.

Oh yes!

You then begin to excavate – delving deeper and deeper into the mound, into history, into our past – and try to uncover, or discover, the truth behind the objects you've unearthed and match them all together.

What you are actually doing is trying to piece together and reveal, in real time, a forgotten or ancient city; a civilization or period in history that you may have only read or heard about and you weren't quite sure whether it had really existed or not.

Thus, a random artefact – a fragment of a goblet, an inscription, or even a crumbling brick wall – becomes a clue that sends you off on a thrilling quest to uncover a long-lost period of history, a forgotten civilization or an ancient city.

And then, when you finally fit all the pieces together – you have a puzzle solved and maybe a lost city found. How awesome is that!

So, now let's find out what exactly makes a city 'lost'.

Our scriptures and ancient texts recount happenings of long, long ago in kingdoms, cities and towns that no longer exist today.

Thus, it was generally believed that they couldn't have happened at all – and those cities never really existed either.

They had to be a figment of somebody's imagination. They had to be stories, myths or legends passed down generations to fire our imagination.

Then, this tribe of experts called archaeologists, armed with their swanky excavation tools, suddenly began unearthing one astonishing piece of evidence after another – suggesting that maybe, just maybe, those cities did exist after all.

At times, they stumbled upon them by accident; at other times, they went looking for them like detectives on a treasure hunt. Guided by old maps and records of fabled cities mentioned in legends and ancient texts – or spurred by rumours or mysterious remnants turning up – they began excavating and finding stonework artefacts and remains of past civilizations from across the world.

They found them buried beneath deserts and oceans, by rivers and atop mountains, within jungles and among ancient ruins.

Soon, physical evidence began popping up everywhere – telling us that we're not the first people to live on Earth. Thousands upon thousands of years ago, long before the time we call history, people had, just as we do today, lived, loved, built homes, danced, fought and enjoyed life – in bustling cities and towns that we hadn't even heard of.

These discoveries showed us what life would or might have been like back then. They also suggested that towns and cities mentioned in legends, scriptures and ancient texts may not be imaginary after all.

Even remnants of whole urbanized cities that weren't mentioned anywhere – not in any book or legend – have popped up.

Once full of life, these ancient inhabitations and civilizations seemed to have been hidden, buried and forgotten for centuries under this mound or that, patiently waiting to be rediscovered.

Thus, such secret places – simply because they were unknown to us until now and 'lost' to us due to ignorance and the passage of time, came to be known as the legendary 'lost cities' of the world.

And because they were secret and unknown, they were also exciting and wrapped in mystery.

They stirred our imagination and filled us with anticipation.

Every ancient stone or artefact unearthed has a story to tell. And those stories entice us and drive us to explore further, dig deeper and discover what the earth may throw up – about the past – from below.

Mankind, you see, has long been fascinated by things that are lost, hidden or mysterious – often exploring and crossing borders to find them.

Driven by various motives, explorers – especially European adventurers – embarked on intrepid journeys to discover the world.

Intrigued by stories of mysterious ruins and unexplored lands, they sailed across seas to discover what lay beyond them.

Along the way, they conquered, colonized, even lost their lives – and yes, also discovered lands that had been lost or unknown to us.

So, was there really a lost city hidden deep in the tangled, treacherous terrains of the Amazon rainforest?

Did explorers looking for it really go missing?

Are there any lost cities submerged beneath the oceans?

Is Dwarka one of them?

Did places like Mohenjo-daro, Takshashila, Pompeii or Machu Picchu – names that evoke mystery and wonder – really exist?

Did people live there?

Yes… and yes – if the experts are to be believed!

And what about Muziris, Poompuhar or even Mamallapuram? Or the many cities from the Indus

Valley Civilization, whose remains and relics have been discovered all across India?

Did they really have connections with Rome?

Were they truly as rich and grand as the stories say?

India, too, has her share of lost cities – shrouded in mystery and waiting to be explored.

If ancient cities like Kashi and Ayodhya in India, or Athens and Rome in Europe, after thousands of years, could still throb with life today, then why have so many others been lost to us?

That is something we'll perhaps never really know.

Even so, thanks to the efforts of archaeologists – not to forget the historians and scientists with their clever tools and cutting-edge technology – we're slowly uncovering more and more secrets of the past, piece by thrilling piece.

The exquisite artefacts and ancient city walls they have uncovered so far give us tantalizing glimpses of a world from long, long ago.

An ancient world of many fascinating cultures and thriving lifestyles – richer and more amazing than anything we could have ever dreamed up.

Of countless kingdoms with their mighty kings and bustling cities, full of people going about their day-to-day lives, that have remained buried, hidden and forgotten for centuries.

Of glorious wars and brave victories, massive destruction and epic defeats that fire the imagination even to this day.

Hidden in mud-filled rubble and water, these places wait patiently for their incredible stories to be told.

Were there really such fabulous places as Shangri-La or El Dorado?

Was one a hidden city–paradise of everlasting youth and the other a dazzling city made of gold?

No one knows for sure – but many brave explorers (and quite a few Indiana Jones–adventurers!) are on the hunt for them.

So, the question arises as to how and why they were lost to us. What great mysteries lie behind their disappearance?

Did aliens destroy them?

Did the earth swallow them whole?

Did the oceans rise and submerge them?

Were they buried, drowned, abandoned – or destroyed in war?

How were they then rediscovered? Who found them? And when?

It would be exciting to find out, wouldn't it?

So, what are we waiting for? Let's go find out, shall we?

Welcome to the world of lost cities.

North
America
South
America
N
W
E
S

1

THE LOST CITY OF Z

When a 'lost' city goes missing...

'We are going to die, Dad,' whispered Jack, his voice breaking. 'We are going to die!'

On their way to discover a lost city deep in the Amazonian rainforests, a place where no outsider had dared to venture, the father-and-son duo had run into a group of hostile, half-naked warriors.

Poison-tipped arrows zinging around them had sent them fleeing for their lives. Then, in the nick of time, a second tribe had appeared on the scene. They drove away the attackers – but had unfortunately then taken the two of them captive.

Sporting feathered headgear and carrying wicked-looking spears, the warriors were a terrifying sight.

They herded Jack and his father into a forest clearing, where a group of elders sat waiting in silence.

A brief exchange between the warriors and the elders had followed.

Then, without a word, a torchlight procession began. Jack and his father were led deeper into the jungle, down a narrow path, flanked by more armed warriors who stared at them with blank, unreadable faces.

Reaching another clearing, the two prisoners were made to kneel, legs tucked tightly beneath them.

They were then made to drink some strange liquid from a carafe. Jack's fear surged. Something deep inside warned him that they might not make it out alive and he told his father so.

As the men around them watched in silence, Jack turned to his father. 'I love you, Dad,' he said quietly. 'I love you too, son,' replied his father, his voice steady but heavy.

Perhaps for the last time.

Just then, someone stepped forward and smeared a strange leafy paste onto their arms and shoulders.

Within minutes, Jack and his father began to feel dizzy. The world around them blurred.

More half-clad warriors appeared.

They gently bore Jack and his father into the darkness of the jungle.

And that was the last the world saw or heard of Lt Col. Percy Fawcett and his son, Jack.

The scene described above is from the 2016 American film *The Lost City of Z*, based on a true story.

“Lieutenant Colonel Percy Harrison Fawcett”

Have you seen it?

It is adapted from journalist David Grann's book (2009) of the same name.

Grann who, eighty years after Percy Fawcett's final expedition into the Amazonian jungle of Mato Grosso in Brazil, set out in 2005 to trace the same route.

He hoped to uncover the mystery behind the disappearance of Fawcett and his son.

Lt Col. Percy Fawcett was a surveyor for the Royal Geographical Society in the United Kingdom. An amateur explorer, he had already made several trips to the Amazon jungle.

On one such trip, he had come across some bits of pottery and ancient relics, which he believed belonged to an amazing lost civilization hidden deep in the Amazon rainforest.

He had also heard many stories and legends about it.

Then, at the National Library of Brazil, he reportedly came across a document – *Manuscript 512* – possibly written by a Portuguese explorer, João da Silva Guimarães, that mentioned an abandoned city deep in the Amazon, filled with vast riches, wide roads, arched buildings and towering statues.

The explorer, however, had been unable to find his way back to this fabulous mysterious place.

Nevertheless, Fawcett was utterly convinced that an incredibly advanced and cultured city lay hidden in the heart of the Amazon jungle – a city no one else knew about!

Fawcett was, however, determined to find it.

Obsessed with the idea, he named it the 'Lost City of Z' and soon set off on a daring expedition to discover it.

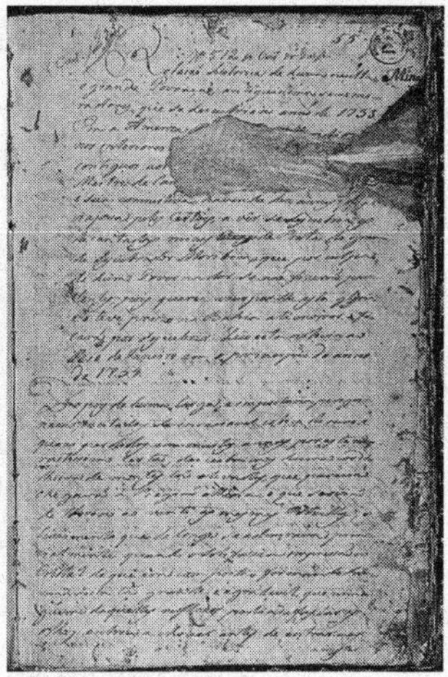

"*A page from* Manuscript 512"

The trip, however, had to be aborted halfway when Fawcett and his group fell ill, forcing him to reluctantly turn back.

Unfortunately for him, after that, there weren't many takers for his theory.

Still, convinced that there was an extraordinary lost city waiting to be found, he decided to go ahead and look for the Lost City of Z on his own.

So, once again, in the summer of 1925, accompanied by Jack, his twenty-two-year-old son, and Raleigh Rimell, Jack's friend, he set out on a journey into the Amazon.

Soon he was sending home detailed dispatches through exhausted runners, describing their Amazonian travails.

These reports caused a media sensation, and the world was fascinated.

However, after about five months of regular updates, the dispatches suddenly stopped.

Although in his last message – from a place he called 'Dead Horse Camp' – he had mentioned that he might be out of contact for a while and hinted at an exciting find, Fawcett was never heard from again.

When news of the Fawcetts' disappearance spread, the world was shocked and intrigued.

Had they been eaten by wild animals?

Were they being held hostage by Brazilian Indians?

Were they killed, starved to death or had they just decided to stay back?

Nobody knew.

Umpteen search parties were sent out, but to no avail.

They had simply vanished without a trace.

Some twenty-five years later, the chief of the Amazonian Kalapalo tribe, while giving details of how Fawcett and his small group had apparently been killed by them, produced a skeleton, claiming it was Fawcett's.

However, the remains turned out to be the bones of the chief's own grandfather.

So, the mystery only deepened.

And no one had any answers.

'They must have gotten lost in the jungle, and starved to death,' said other experienced Amazonian explorers and the Brazilian authorities.

Amazonia – the largest river basin in the world – is notoriously difficult to explore.

Its rainforests span nine South American countries: Brazil, Bolivia, Colombia, Ecuador, Guyana, Peru, Suriname, Venezuela and French Guiana.

Sixty per cent of this expanse lies within Brazil and is home to no fewer than four-hundred ethnic tribes, some of whom are extremely hostile to outsiders.

James Lynch, another Brazilian explorer on the Fawcett trail, was abducted in 1996 and taken prisoner along with eleven members of his team.

By bribing their way out, they barely managed to escape being hung upside down and quartered.

Then there were the venomous serpents, massive anacondas, poisonous plants and dangerous piranhas that had to be avoided just to stay alive.

So, finding anything in the Amazonian wild was not easy.

David Grann, in his search for Fawcett, met with Lynch, and – following what he believed were clues from Fawcett's journals – finally arrived at a village of the Kuikuro people, called Kuhikugu, deep in the Amazonian wilderness, where he met a German explorer-cum-archaeologist, Michael Heckenberger.

Heckenberger had unearthed some twenty ancient settlements in the Xingu River area – exactly where Fawcett had expected to find Z.

Remnants of ancient pottery, defensive ditches around walled cities with round plazas, roads, canals and wooden bridges had all been discovered there.

So, although it was no fabulous city of gold filled with treasures, Grann believed Percy Fawcett had been right after all.

This, Grann told himself, could have been Fawcett's elusive Lost City of Z.

And perhaps the Fawcetts had been killed by an indigenous tribe.

However, there was no definite proof of either.

Even a hundred years later, the mystery of what really happened to the Fawcetts remains unsolved.

Was there yet another undiscovered city of Z – one that Colonel Fawcett believed to be fabulous and hidden deep in the heart of the Amazonian rainforests?

Had he found it before he and his son were killed – if they were killed at all?

Fascinating though it sounds, no one actually knows to this day.

It, however, continues to spark curiosity and awe.

Where is it located: Xingu River region, Amazon rainforest, Brazil
Timeframe of Settlement: 800 CE–1600 CE
Who discovered it and when: Michael Heckenberger in 2003

2

PORT ROYAL

When the earth shakes open...

Let's say you're a seventeenth-century, swashbuckling pirate.

You roam the seas, looting and plundering.

Now, you have so much gold and silver, you need a safe haven.

Where would you go?

You would go to a place where you wouldn't be caught or hanged.

You would go to a place where you would be protected.

Where would that be?

It would be Port Royal in Jamaica.

Yes, Port Royal, known as 'the wickedest city' of the seventeenth century. A harbour town where pirates as

"A portrait of Sir Henry Morgan"

"A drawing of Blackbeard, the pirate"

infamous as Blackbeard and Henry Morgan made their home.

Why was that?

For about 150 years, Port Royal was a Spanish port called Cayo de Carena.

Then the British captured it.

It soon became an even busier and more prosperous trading centre with a British naval base.

Encouraged by the British, seafarers, pirates, buccaneers and other privateers made Port Royal their home.

As they ruthlessly looted Spanish galleons, merchant ships and coastal towns, Port Royal thrived on the money brought in by them.

Port Royal was also the town where auctions of African slaves – brought to work on sugar plantations by British and European slave traders – regularly took place.

Thus, it was home to not just the British Navy but also to a lot of wealthy, rabble-rousing riffraff – planters, merchants, slave traders, drunken sailors, thieves and looters of all races.

It also had many taverns, casinos and sleazy motels, which truly made it a scoundrel's paradise.

Henry Morgan, as notorious as any pirate could be, was once its governor.

It was thus a wealthy, merry old town – but with an extremely shady reputation.

Sadly, however, one fine sunny day, Nature decided to take a call and end it all.

In a matter of seconds, the bustling port became history.

Why? What happened, you might ask…

A massive earthquake – measuring 7.5 on the Richter scale – our good old Earth simply yawned open.

Buildings and people vanished as if into a huge sink hole.

Geysers gushed out from the ground, destroying much of the town.

The soil softened, turned to liquid and slid into the bay.

Fine brick houses toppled and paved roads disappeared.

Within minutes, the heart of Port Royal had been reduced to rubble and quicksand.

Then a tsunami with huge tidal waves rose up to ravage the port.

The swirling waters mounted the wharfs, knocked down the walls of four of its forts, tossed ships onto the streets and swallowed everything in their wake.

Countless other ships in the harbour simply sank, never to sail again.

Thousands lost their lives that day.

So bad was the quake that even graves were flung open – with the turbulent waves washing them clean.

When it finally ended, two-thirds of Port Royal was gone and what was left was a horrendous sight.

A port that once hosted the British Navy and its hero, Admiral Horatio Nelson, had quite simply turned into debris, sand and water.

So, where exactly is Port Royal today?

On a clear day, if you were to peer into the depths of the Caribbean Sea, off the southern coast of Jamaica, you would see, underwater, the contours of the once booming port.

It lies at the end of the Palisadoes, at the mouth of Kingston Harbour in Jamaica, forty feet deep.

Beautiful Jamaica is one of thirteen independent islands that make up the West Indies in the Caribbean.

It was Christopher Columbus from Spain who first discovered Jamaica and Port Royal.

"A portrait of a man said to be Christopher Columbus"

He had come hoping to find his way to India.

And a city in Jamaica – Cayo de Carena, as it was called then – was where he first dropped anchor.

He believed it was the west of India and so 'West Indies' the group of islands became.

With a natural harbour that was a safe dockyard for ships that needed repairs or services, it was strategically placed on the Atlantic-Caribbean trade routes.

So it was that the British, who had their eye on the port city for a while, invaded Jamaica, defeated the Spanish and seized control of it.

Renaming Cayo de Carena as Port Royal, they then turned it into a well-fortified, flourishing pirate republic.

After all it did make for an ideal launching pad for attacks on French ships, Spanish vessels and towns on the coast, didn't it?

And those who did that were even welcomed back with gun salutes.

Port Royal, however, was a disaster waiting to happen.

Built on sand and silt deposits washed into the Caribbean from rivers in the Blue Mountains, it lay vulnerable, constantly battered by tidal waves and hurricanes.

Over time, its foundations gradually weakened, and when the earth shook violently, as it did that day, the soil turned soft, liquefied – and flowed into the harbour.

So too did every structure, man, woman and child that stood upon it.

A 1686-pocket watch, recovered nearly three centuries later in 1969, had stopped at exactly 11.43 a.m.

Could it have been on the seventh of June 1692, when the earthquake struck and the port vanished into the sea?

Perhaps.

The British then tried to gradually rebuild Port Royal.

It no longer played host to scoundrels and pirates.

Many pirates were executed, and honest trade was encouraged.

The naval station was also upgraded.

However, another massive earthquake in 1907 – 6.5 on the Richter scale – along with a series of other quakes, hurricanes, fires and tidal waves soon finished off the port.

UNESCO tells us that up to 1994, Port Royal – or what was left of it – has been battered by no less than forty-seven hurricanes, nine earthquakes and two major fires.

Twenty years on, even more such disasters have occurred.

While the once-pirate-capital of Jamaica is still lost and underwater, what is left of it is just another little sleepy coastal fishing village where marine archaeologists and tourists roam.

Underwater investigations and attempts to rebuild the sunken city, however, are still ongoing.

Where is it located: Jamaica, West Indies
Timeframe of Settlement: 1494 CE–1692 CE
Who discovered it and when: Institute of Nautical Archaeology, Texas A&M University and the Jamaica National Heritage Trust between 1981–1990

3

EL DORADO

When greed fuels an imaginary lost city...

The man looked ethereal. He glittered.

Plastered from head to toe in fine gold dust, he walked erect, with an almost otherworldly calm.

Though stark naked, not an inch of bare skin or strand of hair was visible beneath the powdered gold.

Then, in a sombre procession led by priests adorned in golden feathers, he stepped onto a gleaming raft, gilded and heavy with sparkling artefacts.

As the riverbank filled with chanting crowds, the golden raft slowly sailed along to the centre of the lake.

When it stopped, the glittering man stood tall, surrounded by the golden-feathered holy men. With quiet reverence, he offered the gold and treasures on his raft to the deep, dark water below.

Then into the lake, dove the man of gold himself.

As he came up for air, devoid of all the powdered gold, the spectators tittered in excitement.

Throwing in their own gold and precious gems as offerings into the lake, they hailed their new chief – their new king – as he then, majestically sailed back to shore.

Some of the sixteenth-century tribes – in particular the Muiscas – deep in the forests of South America, appointed or coronated their new leaders in a similar fashion.

With so much gold on show, it was a mesmerizing sight – especially for those who valued gold as wealth.

“Musica raft or the Golden Raft of El Dorado at the Gold Museum, Bogotá, Colombia”

Hence, it began to attract greedy European explorers who were out sailing the seas, exploring new places and coveting riches to take back to their own countries.

'Where could all this gold have come from?' they wondered. 'It had to have had a source.'

Rumours began to spread about lakes filled with treasure, temples of solid gold and, finally, an entire city of gold and vast riches hidden deep in the Andes.

Indeed, a whole city of gold filled with treasures, untold and unfound.

How rich would they be if only they could lay their hands on it.

The very thought excited them.

And so began the race for the South American city of gold.

First came the sixteenth-century Spanish explorers.

Then soon, from all across the rest of Europe, they flocked.

Notwithstanding the dangers, they trudged, trampled and sailed from Colombia to Bogotá to Peru – wherever they believed this city of vast riches might lie.

"A portrait of Francisco de Orellana"

One Francisco de Orellana, an explorer from

Spain, discovered instead the massive river Amazon, along which he sailed for months until he reached the Atlantic.

Of the city of gold, however, there was not a sign.

They dragged the lakes, dug up wells, robbed the local tribes and seized whatever gold they could – and there was a fair amount to loot – but the city of gold they so desperately coveted was still nowhere to be found.

Yet, stories abounded and rumours spread of a mysterious city of gold, so rich it boggled the mind.

The South American cities of the Amazon were indeed rich – but their gold was never meant to enrich themselves.

“A portrait of Sir Walter Raleigh”

Crafted from *tumbaga*, an alloy of gold, silver and copper, their artefacts were ceremonial, made solely for sacred rituals to honour their gods.

The greedy explorers, however – ready to murder, pillage and burn for even a glint of it – took whatever treasures they could find, wherever they could find them.

They remained convinced that even greater riches lay hidden somewhere deep within the vast Amazon rainforest.

Why, even the famous Sir Walter Raleigh came – not once but many times – only to return disappointed.

A nobleman and explorer in the court of the English Queen Elizabeth I and her successor, Sir Walter was obsessed with finding the golden city.

Sadly, his search for the golden city came at a terrible cost. The Spanish killed his son. And back home, Raleigh himself was executed for defying royal orders to not provoke and get into a conflict with the Spanish – who, of course, were hunting for the same treasures.

Still, they searched, day after day, year after year.

Many drowned. Many fell ill. Many never returned.

Yet, excited and ever hopeful, they continued to sail down the Amazon's winding rivers, hacking through dense swathes of jungle, braving poisonous arrows, venomous snakes and stinging scorpions – all in a fruitless search for this elusive city of glittering jewels and unimaginable riches.

Then came the Spanish conquistador – meaning conqueror and soldier – Sebastián de Belalcázar who first spoke of *El Dorado*. Now, El Dorado in Spanish means the 'gilded one' or 'the golden one', so, he wasn't perhaps referring to a place, but to the man anointed in gold during the sacred coronation ritual at the lake. Over time, the meaning blurred, and *El Dorado* soon came to mean not just a man, but a city – a place of endless gold. And so, the myth grew.

El Dorado soon became a fabled kingdom hidden deep in the jungle, where even its king was said to be covered in gold. It became a city of gold that simply had to be found.

However, where exactly was this mysterious glittering place? Even after four-hundred years, no one knows for sure.

It continues to remain lost, and elusive – if it ever truly existed at all.

Still, who knows with today's cutting-edge technology and AI – Artificial Intelligence – perhaps the mythical El Dorado might just pop up someday.

Until then, it continues to fascinate, intrigue and fuel the imagination of the world.

Where is it located: A mythical place in South America
Timeframe of Settlement: Sixteenth century CE (imaginary)
Who discovered it and when: Explorers are still looking

4

MACHU PICCHU

Not quite so lost...

Would you like to go to Machu Picchu?

It's one of the most famous and fascinating ancient cities in Peru – once lost to the world.

Yes, it lies deep in the forests and high up in the Andes Mountains, but it is no longer lost and if you ever visit, you certainly won't regret it.

Just follow the Inca trail, the same route that American Yale University professor and explorer Hiram Bingham took in 1911 while searching for the fabled lost city of Vilcabamba in South America.

Vilcabamba, Bingham believed, was the lost golden capital of the Incas – indigenous South American people, and he was determined to find it.

So, guided by locals and hacking his way through Peru's dense, snake-infested jungles for days, he finally fetched up at what he believed was Vilcabamba.

However, it was not Vilcabamba – the legendary lost city of the Incas – but a far more exciting place he had stumbled upon.

He had, by sheer accident, landed up at Machu Picchu – an extraordinary hidden terrace city, ensconced between two peaks, some 80 km up in the Andes Mountains. It lay between Machu (old) Picchu (peak) and the Huayna (new) Picchu (peak).

With some 200 amazing buildings in white, built on different levels with terraces that grew crops, vegetables and fruits, it had no less than a dozen fountains, temples, residences and a fabulous winter palace.

Open to the skies, it also had a remarkable solar clock or calendar, cut out of a single Intihuatana granite stone, that marked the summer and winter solstice.

Carved out of the sides of the mountain and hidden from view, Machu Picchu was a settlement of the royals that no one in the world knew about.

"Intihuatana (solar clock) at Machu Picchu"

Sure, a few locals had vaguely heard about it, but since they hadn't seen it, they didn't know whether it was a myth or not.

It had thus remained lost and undiscovered for more than 500 years.

Built by King Pachacuti of the Incas, it was his secret retreat where he holidayed every winter with his royal entourage.

Bingham didn't know that the actual Vilcabamba – discovered later – was about 80 km away.

Pachacuti's Inca empire was vast.

His capital, Cusco, was an unbelievably rich and beautiful city with palaces, temples and fountains.

Connected by many small roads, Cusco had some main highways along the coast and the Andes Mountains.

A well-hidden path led to Machu Picchu as well.

And Machu Picchu, the palace retreat he had built for himself, was no less gorgeous.

Amongst fields and fields of 90–300 varieties of colourful orchids with butterflies and parrots fluttering around, it was a slice of heaven on earth.

Machu Picchu, however, had probably been rocked by earthquakes quite often.

You see, its buildings had some amazing interlocking white granite blocks that bounced during earthquakes and fell back into place later, to prevent buildings from collapsing.

What was fantastic was they were still standing despite centuries of earthquakes. The engineering skills of the Inca engineers and builders were quite remarkably astonishing, don't you think?

Cusco's highways had some incredible tunnels, bridges, storehouses and rest stops for travellers too.

Can you imagine all this and more, as long ago as some 600 years ago?

Such stunning expertise so many centuries ago is what perhaps surprised the world.

Now, the Incas also had vast amounts of gold and silver, more than anybody could dream of.

They simply mined it off the sides of the Andes Mountains. Thus, its fame as a wealthy empire spread across the world.

Very soon, along came Francisco Pizarro from Spain, greedy for all that gold.

However, by the time the Spaniard came calling, Pachacuti had died, and among those who followed him was an emperor named Atahualpa, who had made the empire even more prosperous.

Now, this Pizarro had guns, he had horses and also two-hundred soldiers, known as the Spanish Conquistadors (or conquerors), in metal armour, who soon decimated the vast Inca army.

Fighting on foot with swords, and bows and arrows, they were no match for the marauding Spanish.

Pizarro demanded that Atahualpa give him as much gold and silver as he desired.

Atahualpa did.

Although the emperor fulfilled Pizarro's every wish, Pizarro still killed him, melted all the gold, split it amongst

Pizarro Seizing the Inca of Peru, painting by John Everett Millais (1846)

his men, demolished the entire Inca empire and attempted to colonize it.

The Incas had, until then, lived a sheltered existence within the forests of South America.

Isolated from the outside world, they hadn't been exposed to its diseases.

Before long, smallpox, a dreaded disease – hitherto unknown to the Incas but rampant elsewhere – spread and wiped out more than half the Inca population.

It was around that time, perhaps due to its inconvenient location, that Machu Picchu, about a hundred years after it was first built, was also abandoned.

The Spanish, too, never found it or even knew it existed because no one had told them about it.

Hence, with no emperors visiting and, in time, not even his nobles going there, either there was no one to live in Machu Picchu or even remember where it was.

The forests soon took over and completely covered it with vegetation, and Machu Picchu went into a decline.

So, unseen and forgotten, it became completely unknown.

However, now Bingham, thrilled by the idea of having found what he mistakenly believed was the city of Vilcabamba, wrote a book on it.

His *Lost City of the Incas* caused a sensation.

It caused such excitement the world over that soon busloads of explorers were wending their way to discover this lost city.

Bingham was not even the first one to discover the lost city of Machu Picchu that he mistakenly believed to be Vilcabamba.

There was one Lizárraga before him. A Peruvian explorer-farmer, he had, nine years earlier, carved his name, 'A. Lizárraga 1902', on one of the rocks.

However, Bingham, on spotting it, reportedly ignored it and, to the great delight of the public and the media, made it his life's mission to publicize the lost city – he mistakenly believed was Vilcabamba – as his own discovery.

It was not until 1964, when the famous Peruvian explorer Gene Savoy identified another place, 'Espíritu Pampa', as Vilcabamba, did everyone realize that it was not Vilcabamba but Machu Picchu that Bingham had discovered, by which time, in 1956, Bingham had died.

And if you do go up there, don't miss the llamas and alpacas still grazing calmly among the ruins spread over 80 km.

"Hiram Bingham III at his desk in 1917"

Some 3,000 steps will take you to different terrace levels that will fill your lungs with pure oxygen beneath an often brilliant, rainbow-lit sky.

Thus, for a happy adventure, you will do no better than spectacular Machu Picchu, abandoned perhaps and hidden from view but not quite lost.

Where is it located: Near River Urubamba in Cusco Valley, Andes, Peru

Timeframe of Settlement: 1450 CE–1565 CE

Who discovered it and when: Agustín Lizárraga in 1902; Hiram Bingham in 1911

5

ROANOKE

When whole settlements disappear...

Four-hundred-and-thirty-seven years ago, 115 people on an island simply disappeared off the face of the earth.

One year here; three years later – gone.

Could they have relocated elsewhere?

No, no evidence of that.

Could they have drowned, or been killed by perhaps tsunamis or storms, volcanoes or earthquakes – natural calamities as we have seen so far?

No, absolutely no evidence of that.

Could they then have perhaps fallen victim to warring tribes?

No sign of that either, or of anything else.

Yet it happened.

How did it happen? Why did it happen?

Nobody, to this day, knows.

It happened during the reign of Elizabeth I of England.

England was busy establishing colonies across the world.

English ships roamed the globe exploring and trading, with Sir Walter Raleigh at the helm.

Raleigh, a nobleman and courtier in the court of Queen Elizabeth I, was also an adventurer at heart.

From El Dorado to the colonies of North America, he spearheaded British expeditions.

So, in 1584, to reconnoitre the 'New World', which was North America, he sent out a ship.

Their mission: to find a suitable site to set up an English colony or trading post.

So, to Roanoke Island they went.

They met up with a few local Native Americans who went back to England with them.

Hearing what they had to say, Raleigh decided it was as good a place as any for an English settlement.

So, in 1585, a second lot of five ships with a hundred and seven settlers under Captain Grenville, made their way there.

They made themselves quite comfortable and built themselves a large fort as well.

However, food and supplies soon ran out, so Grenville set sail for home, promising to return quickly with more people and provisions.

Unfortunately, he was unable to do so.

So, two years later, in 1587, Raleigh sent another group of colonists under John White to check on the settlers left behind in Roanoke.

They did, but, barring a skeleton, there was no sign of them.

Some of them, they were told later, may have made their way back home to England.

However, nobody knew for sure.

John White was a talented mapmaker who had taken part in other expeditions too. So, undeterred, he decided to stay and re-establish the colony.

Thus, was born the first permanent English settlement in North America.

Around 117 Englishmen, women and children made their homes on Roanoke Island that year.

This time round, however, the locals were unfriendly and hostile.

The weather was unkind, the winter harsh.

Soon, supplies ran short, and their safety too became a problem. Setting up home and defending themselves from the local tribes was thus proving to be difficult.

John White then reluctantly decided to go back to England and return with reinforcements.

He left behind his daughter, son-in-law and infant granddaughter, who was born there.

She was the first English child to be born in the 'New World'.

'If anything were to happen to you or you are forced to relocate,' White ordered, 'leave a coded message for me – a cross if there is danger or the name of the place you go to.'

And off went White, home to England.

As luck would have it, he couldn't get back to Roanoke for the next three years.

You see, war had broken out between Spain and England. So, there were no ships to take him back to Roanoke.

King Philip of Spain had gathered a great fleet of his best and largest warships, famously known as the Spanish Armada, and, in 1588, sailed into the English Channel, to invade and conquer England.

However, the English were waiting, and, in one of the most famous battles in British history, the English defeated the Spanish.

So, White, unable to return to Roanoke as promised – due to the war – could only go back in 1590, three years later.

And when he did, he was stunned to find no one there.

It was both shocking and mysterious.

The entire colony of 115 people had quite simply vanished. There was no sign of his daughter, his little granddaughter or any of the others left behind.

There were no signs of battle.

There were no bodies or skeletons.

The fort, however, had been dismantled, as were the houses.

Yet, it all looked orderly, with no hint of why the place was deserted.

There were, however, two clues:

The word 'CROATOAN' carved into a wooden post, and 'CRO' engraved on the trunk of a tree nearby.

“John White finds the message ‘CROATOAN’ at the abandoned Roanoke Colony”

There was no sign of a cross next to either.

Now Croatoan, 80 km away, was a friendly neighbouring island, known today as Hatteras Island.

So, White deduced that the people may have relocated there.

He decided to set sail for the island of Croatoan, but severe storms made him turn homewards to England instead.

He vowed to return as soon as the weather settled.

However, he couldn’t, and nobody went back to Roanoke until 1609 – nineteen years later.

And when they did, it was the same deserted town with no one in it.

About ninety men, fifteen women and ten children remained lost. They had simply vanished.

Where could they all have gone?

Had they relocated to Croatoan as per the clue?

So now to Croatoan he went, searching for the Roanoke settlers.

However, no signs of any English settlers were found there.

They were perhaps twenty years too late.

Could they have split up into smaller groups and dispersed?

Again, no evidence was found in any of the islands nearby either.

Could they have, since no reinforcements came, integrated with the locals in the years that followed?

Even if they did, wouldn't someone from Roanoke have remembered their origins?

Yet no one did.

Could the Spanish, who were always at loggerheads with the English, have wiped them out?

The Spanish themselves, in 1600 CE, sent people to look for the Roanoke colonists.

Would they have done so if they had been responsible for their disappearance?

Over the years, many expeditions have been launched to uncover the fate of the British settlement in Roanoke.

However, all have been to no avail.

Then came the archaeologists.

In 1998, four-hundred years later, they found some English farthings – coins – and a ring they believed could have belonged to one of the Roanoke colonists, possibly someone named Kendall.

It could have been washed up during high tide or a storm at any time, they said, so the discovery was discounted.

Then some carvings on stones, supposedly by Eleanor Dare, daughter of John White, came to light.

These too, however, were dismissed as spurious.

Between 2016 and 2023, archaeologists discovered sixteenth-century fragments of an English apothecary jar, tools and other pottery shards.

Yet none of this explained what had happened to the Roanoke settlers.

The mystery of Roanoke, therefore, continues to mystify.

It remains one of the world's great unsolved mysteries.

Where is it located: North Carolina, USA
Timeframe of Settlement: 1587 CE–1590 CE
Who discovered it and when: Unknown

6

LA CIUDAD PERDIDA

When searching for a lost city...

In South America's Colombia lies the Sierra Nevada de Santa Marta.

One of the world's highest coastal mountain ranges, it is at least 18,700 feet high.

And it is a range like no other.

Unusual and intriguing, it is filled with mysterious lost cities.

To find them however is another matter.

Choked with dense forests and heavy vegetation, it is every explorer's nightmare.

So, wait – how are they 'lost' if we know about them?

We didn't, until LiDAR came along.

LiDAR – short for **Li**ght **D**etection **a**nd **R**anging – is a remote-sensing device mounted on aircrafts and drones. It fires hundreds of thousands of infrared pulses (or beams) per second towards the ground, and when each beam strikes anything on Earth's surface, it bounces back with a measure of the distance.

The vast amount of data it produces is automatically fed into a computer, and before you know it, you have high-resolution images from which you can digitally remove all the vegetation, leaving just the archaeological remains if any.

It creates detailed 3D maps that reveal the layout of the land and any ancient human-made structures not normally visible to us.

Now, half of the world's rainforests lie in the Amazon in South America, and Colombia makes up about 10 per cent of that.

So, you can imagine the fun today's explorers – unlike those in the past – might have with such super powerful new technology.

So, the Amazon rainforests soon became the go-to place for all scientists and archaeologists.

No longer impenetrable, they became their playground.

And that is how *National Geographic* magazine explorer Albert Lin and archaeologist Santiago Giraldo, who had been scoping the region for lost cities for years, spotted something unbelievably beautiful.

On a flyby they saw plateau-like clusters of land, wrapped in dense vegetation, bursting forth into the skyline from the Sierra Nevada de Santa Marta.

It was the city of La Ciudad Perdida.

Stone paths or tracks led out from the city in every direction.

There was also an entrance with a slablike stone map filled with markings.

Could they be the various routes to and from that place?

'If they followed those tracks, would they lead to another lost city?' they wondered.

Now, La Ciudad Perdida had actually been discovered a while earlier – back in 1972.

Thieves had long known that such ancient sites, especially their tombs, were often filled with valuable gold artefacts buried alongside the ancient dead.

So, one day, when some hungry looters, chasing a turkey, stumbled onto some stone stairs hidden among thick vegetation, they realized they had found the remains of a settlement – a town with well-laid-out ruins and tombs, hidden among the gnarled trees and stubbly roots.

It was La Ciudad Perdida.

Earlier known as Teyuna, it was the heart of a network of villages belonging to the Tairona people.

Built along the Buritaca River, it was first known as Green Hell, then Buritaca-200, and later *La Ciudad Perdida,* meaning 'lost city' in Spanish.

Research suggests that Ciudad Perdida dates back to between 600 and 800 CE.

An engineering marvel, it was built on a human-made plateau high in the mountains.

It even had an in-built drainage system to protect itself from the Amazon's relentless rains.

An urbanized society, the Tairona also seemed to have excelled in metallurgy (or metalwork).

Exquisite gold ornaments and intricate artefacts revealed a level of craftsmanship rarely seen before.

La Ciudad Perdida's discovery had caused a sensation.

Thieves swarmed to the site to loot its tombs, sell the plunder to the outside world and fill their pockets.

Soon, Europe's museums began to boast of ancient artefacts of gold and silver looted from the Amazon's latest lost city.

So, when Lin and Giraldo went exploring, hoping to see if more cities like La Ciudad Perdida existed, their LiDAR – perched on a helicopter – not only revealed new features of Perdida itself but also, to their delight, uncovered some amazing, previously unseen structures nearby.

The digital 3D model of the area around Ciudad Perdida showed similar, but until-then hidden, man-made flat surfaces carved into the slopes that, yes, looked like a separate city.

Intrigued, they decided to confirm it physically.

They followed the digital map created by the lasers and climbed the man-made plateau they had spotted – despite the thick foliage.

Battling poisonous snakes, stinging scorpions and thorny bushes along the way, it was a punishing, 32 km-ascent through steep terrain and dense jungle.

When they found pieces of pottery shards, terracing and stonework from yet another mysterious, forgotten and hitherto-unknown city, they were thrilled beyond belief.

What was even more exciting was that this city had been left untouched and unplundered.

So far, further six ancient settlement sites have been identified.

Experts believe there could be nearly 600 more.

This new find – still unnamed – appears to have been inhabited by the same Tairona people, a mysterious but highly advanced civilization.

Now the Kogi people – likely descendants of the Tairona – who live along the coast, say the Tairona thrived for thousands of years until the Spanish conquistadors arrived and made their lives hell.

The Spaniards were interested only in looting the Tairona of their gold and colonizing them.

The Tairona, skilled professionals – engineers and warriors – put up a spirited resistance against the Spanish invaders but were ultimately driven out of their homes.

Many escaped into the mountains, many were enslaved and many died of diseases brought in by the European invaders.

Slowly, the once-peaceful settlement began to disintegrate – perhaps during the sixteenth century.

The descendants of the Tairona, like the Kogi, are now said to be spread throughout the Sierra Nevada de Santa Marta.

Today, a network of stone-tiled pathways, spiralling stairs, walls and about 169 rounded terraces covered in moss are all that remain of the once-vibrant city of La Ciudad Perdida.

However, this ancient city – that once lay abandoned and lost behind tagua palms, rampaging vines and overgrown bushes for centuries – was a significant find for Colombia.

It even features on the country's 50-peso currency note.

Now, it's also a tourist attraction that's raking in the pesos.

Efforts are also underway to discover the name of the city found near La Ciudad Perdida.

But for LiDAR, wouldn't such lost cities still remain lost to us?

Where is it located: Northwestern Colombia, South America

Timeframe of Settlement: Seventh century CE–Sixteenth century

Who found it and when: Los Sepúlveda family (looters) between 1970–1972

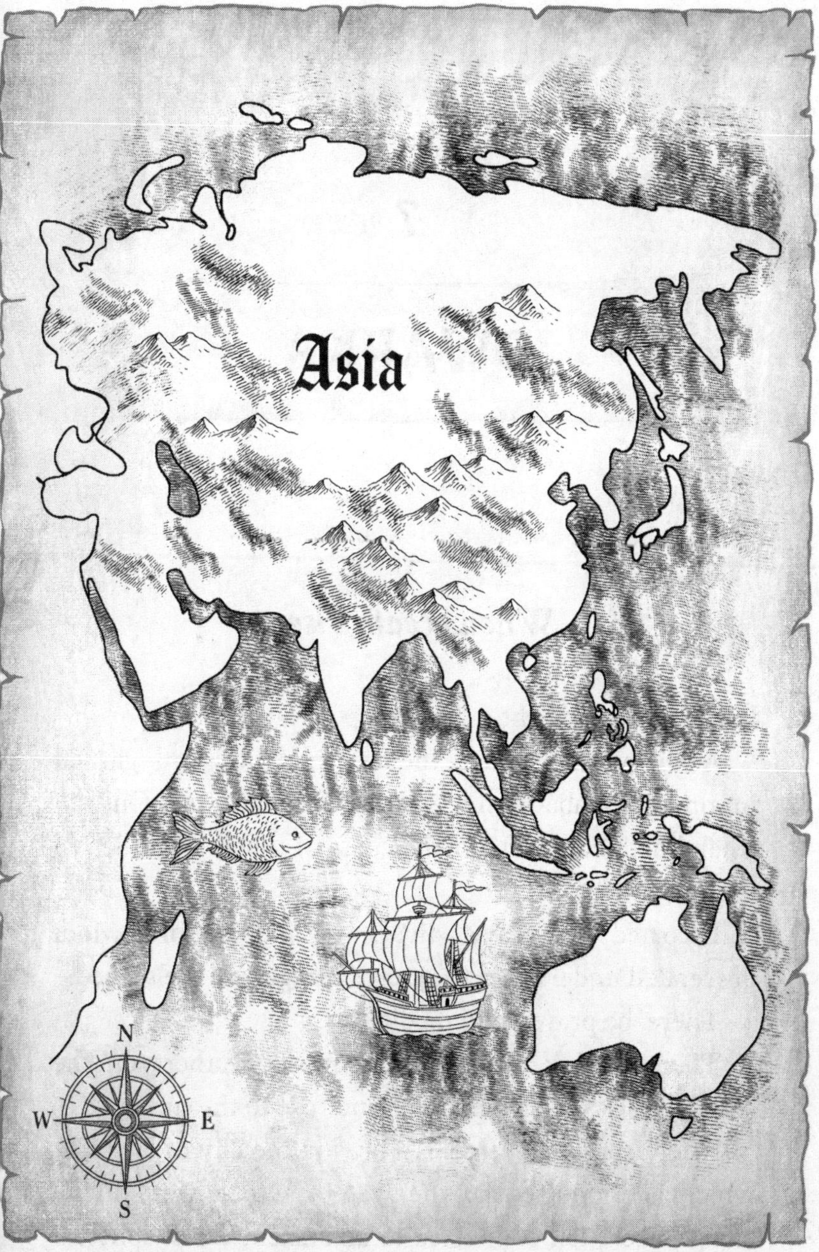
Asia
N
W
E
S

7

DWARKA

When oceans rise...

It was a strange sight.

As the world watched, India's prime minister – garbed in orange scuba-diving gear – slid into the Gulf of Khambhat (Cambay), off the coast of the Arabian Sea in Gujarat, India.

Escorted by Navy divers, Shri Narendra Modi descended underwater to sit cross-legged on the seabed.

There, he prayed and meditated.

Then, placing a bundle of peacock feathers on the seabed, he offered a namaskar and rose to the surface.

After that, he tweeted, 'To pray in the city of Dwarka, which is immersed in the waters, was a very divine experience. I felt connected to an ancient era of spiritual grandeur and timeless devotion. May Bhagwan Shri Krishna bless us all.'

And suddenly, as eminent archaeologist S.R. Rao put it, 'myth just became reality.'

Why was that?

Well, because some thousands of years ago – according to Hindu mythology – in the time of the great epic Mahabharata, just after the great war, Lord Krishna said to Arjuna, 'It's time for me to leave this world. Dwarka will then be taken over by the sea. Before that happens, please have my people evacuated.'

Now, is Lord Krishna the same naughty, butter-loving little boy from Mathura and Brindavan – ancient towns in present-day Uttar Pradesh?

Yes, he was the very same child from Hindu mythology, born to kill his wicked uncle, who later grew up to become the founder and king of Dwarka.

He was also an advisor and friend of his cousin Arjuna – one of the Pandava princes who fought his Kaurava cousins over the kingdom of Hastinapur in the Mahabharata War.

And Krishna was an avatar of Lord Vishnu, wasn't he? Which is why he could foresee what was to come.

Soon after, Krishna, struck by a hunter's arrow, passed away.

And Arjuna rushed to Dwarka.

He gathered whoever he could and hustled them out of the city.

Supposedly designed by the divine architect, Vishwakarma, Dwarka was a stupendously wealthy city –

with golden gates and hundreds of well-laid palaces studded with sapphires, emeralds and rubies.

It was the capital of Krishna's kingdom – and truly one of a kind.

Krishna, determined to escape from Magadha's King Jarasandha's constant attacks, had asked the sea god for some land far away from his home in Mathura (in present-day Uttar Pradesh).

The sea god obliged and on land reclaimed from the sea – near a town called Kushasthali, where the river Gomti meets the Arabian sea on the western coast in today's Gujarat – Krishna led his people, the Yadavas, and established his kingdom.

And there, it had flourished for many years.

Now, as he began to leave, Arjuna turned to take one last look at Krishna's divine city – and what he saw stayed with him forever.

He saw the ocean rise as one – and before his very eyes, Dwarka was no more.

Gone were the gardens, the exquisite palaces, the graceful boulevards, the sparkling fountains.

Within minutes, the sea had swallowed every piece of land and building that had once formed Krishna's magnificent kingdom.

All that remained was a calm expanse of water, where white-rimmed waves rippled endlessly.

And there, beneath the sea, it is believed, Krishna's Dwarka lay hidden for the next five thousand odd years.

Now Hindu mythology also throws up yet another version of the story.

It says there was a fierce aerial battle – with aliens or extraterrestrials in spaceships – or vimanas – after which Krishna's kingdom later sank into the same sea.

No guesses as to which story you would like to believe.

Anyway, the real question is, did Krishna's Dwarka truly exist?

Was it simply a part of Hindu mythology – or a real, thriving kingdom?

Could the waters of the Arabian Sea actually be hiding something so precious, so divine?

Nobody knows for sure.

Followers of Hinduism, however, believe it did exist.

And that belief has long intrigued archaeologists, geologists and historians alike.

So, these experts went looking.

What they discovered was that as time went by, the sea around Dwarka would often recede and rise again.

As a result, over the centuries, about eight different settlements appear to have thrived in and around modern-day Dwarka town and the Dwarkadhish temple that stood on the shore.

They would flourish for a while and then submerge again.

Normal sea erosion or geological changes along with high tides, they say, were the reasons.

Present-day Dwarka is probably the latest of such avatars.

It was, however, a Dwarka rebuilt several times with no sign of Krishna's Dwarka ever popping up, unless in legends.

Once a booming port, its very name *Dwarka* meant, 'Gateway.'

Like a sentinel, though looted over the centuries – multiple times – first by Muslim rulers and later the British, the ancient five storeyed Dwarkadhish temple reportedly built by Vajranabha, one of Lord Krishna's great-grandsons, continues to stand tall on the shore.

Now, about 30 km north of present-day Dwarka, at the mouth of the Gulf of Kutch, lies the island of Bet Dwarka – and it is around this area that it is now believed Krishna's famous sunken abode may have flourished.

A painting of Dwarka in the late 1820s, by William Purser

It was where – Hindu texts tell us – Krishna probably resided, while the rest of Dwarka was the kingdom he administered.

It was said to have been at least 84 km wide before it submerged and was lost to the world.

The very first marine excavations, almost ninety-five years ago, excited our scientists and set the ball rolling.

Some ancient stone tools and pieces of pottery were found.

Then, some thirty years later, came more thrilling evidence: 30 to 40 km from the shore, traces of an ancient city covering a large area of the seabed were picked up.

Fortified walls, stone blocks, pillars and stone anchors were discovered.

Then more evidence emerged.

Oceanographers from India's National Institute of Ocean Technology on a routine pollution-study expedition in the Gulf of Khambhat sent down beams of sound waves using side scan sonar – from the other side of the bay – to the bottom of the ocean and what they found stunned them.

At a depth of 120 feet, were huge geometrical structures that resembled a city, 7–8 km long and 3–4 km wide, with huge pillars and a massive human-made wall nearly 550 m in length.

Many ancient artefacts – including conch shells, temple bells and copper vessels also – lay strewn across the ocean floor.

Researchers were convinced that these were the remnants of a lost city.

Main Dwarka they however feel still lies submerged, about 2–3 km below the ocean bed.

So, even if we choose to believe that the Mahabharata and other ancient Hindu texts are purely mythological, how then do we explain the discoveries made by scientists and marine archaeologists?

So, this lost city could very well be part of Krishna's kingdom, Dwarka, couldn't it?

And that is why the Prime Minister of India decided to do what he did.

So, could it be that the most divine of all cities, Dwarka, is in the process of being rediscovered?

It's a fascinating thought, isn't it – that a kingdom and city believed to be a myth and steeped in legend and mystery for so long, may have actually existed thousands of years ago?

Future marine excavations will tell us more and perhaps a divine mystery will finally be solved.

How awesome is that!

Where is it located: Gulf of Kutch and Gulf of Khambhat, off the western coast of India

Timeframe of Settlement: Third millennium BCE–1500 BCE

Who discovered it and when:

ASI began work in 1930s

8

PETRA

When rockfaces chip and crumble...

Johann Ludwig Burckhardt was a Swiss citizen.

Now, however, disguised as an Arab, he was in Syria and on his way to the tomb of Aaron – brother of Moses in the Bible.

It was rumoured to lie in an ancient lost city somewhere between Aleppo and Cairo, and the last European explorer who went looking for the lost city had been murdered.

Burckhardt, however, was not to be deterred.

Travelling through Damascus and Amman, Burckhardt eventually reached Kerak.

But no sooner had he left the town of Kerak that his guide ran away, leaving him with nothing but the clothes on his back.

Still undeterred, Burckhardt pressed on until he chanced upon a Bedouin camp, with nomadic Arab people.

Chatting them up he got himself a new guide and resumed his journey.

Soon, he found himself in the middle of a vast desert – once a Roman province, now a harsh and forgotten stretch of Arabia.

He had entered an area called Petraea – where Moses had supposedly struck a rock to bring forth water for the Israelites.

As they neared the Wadi Musa or the Valley of Moses, where Moses's brother Aaron's tomb was rumoured to lie.

'Could I sacrifice a goat there?' Burckhardt asked his guide in true Arab fashion.

The guide nodded and silently led him through a narrow, winding gorge called the 'Siq'.

“*Johann Ludwig Burckhardt*”

And then – did Burckhardt walk into an astounding sight or what?

A sight that simply took his breath away.

Before him were some of the most spectacular, architectural wonders he could have ever hoped to see.

Carved into the pink sandstone rock face of

the mountains was a magnificent collection of sculpted columns, arches and doorways.

One in particular – the *Al-Khazneh* or Treasury – a royal tomb crowned with an urn, left him utterly stunned.

Remember the hiding place in *Indiana Jones and the Last Crusade* or in *The Mummy Returns*? This was it.

Beyond it, half-buried in shifting sands was an even more astonishing array of tombs, monuments and apartments, all chiselled out of rose-coloured sandstone cliffs.

He found innumerable alcoves, statues, altars, shrines and – believc it or not – a theatre.

“ Theatre found in Petra ”

With winding pathways, stairways and water channels, it even had a swimming pool.

Cut along the natural curves of the cliffs, gorges and canyons, it was a gorgeous city.

A city that seemed like it had grown out of the pink-and-white cliffs.

This must be the lost city, he told himself – the city of Petra, where no European has ever been.

Petra – the city that, according to the Bible, the ancient Israelites were always warring with.

Although he hadn't found the tomb, he got back to his civilization and let the world know of his astounding discovery.

Soon historians and archaeologists set to work.

They discovered that it was indeed Petra.

Ancient Petra was once the capital of a vast and powerful empire ruled by the Nabataeans, a nomadic desert people.

The Nabataeans had carved out an oasis of trade and craft from the mountain cliffs and canyons, with more than enough food and water for their needs.

With one half jutting out and the other embedded in the rock, *Petra* – meaning 'rock' in Greek – was built on a terrace, carved from east to west along the Wadi Musa, or the Valley of Moses.

In an amazing network of rock-cut channels, canals, underground cisterns, springs and fountains spread across the city, the Nabataeans had managed to efficiently store, connect and distribute water in a barren, sterile desert, where there had been none. Remarkably, some of those cisterns are still in use today.

Amidst the barren cliffs and sands, Petra stood out as an engineering marvel.

Two-thousand-years ago, Petra had essentially been a flourishing trading hub.

Caravans passing through, stopped to rest, paid a toll and carried on.

As demand for goods and traffic to and from Asia, Arabia and Africa increased, so did Petra's importance.

Visitors from China, Greece and Egypt too flocked to the city for cultural exchanges.

Petra connected Southern Arabia with Europe.

Attracted by its wealth and popularity, the Romans then invaded Petra.

For the next three centuries or so, Petra had become a part of the Roman Empire.

Gradually, as maritime trade routes were discovered, Petra's importance as a trading hub began to decline.

Then came the Christians.

Emperor Constantine I's strong faith in Christ led Rome to embrace Christianity – as did the rest of the empire, including Petra.

Churches sprang up, Christian saints were revered, and the old gods were abandoned – for the next three centuries and more.

Petra was then rocked by a series of earthquakes.

The city of the rose-coloured rock face began to crumble.

Buildings chiselled by hand out of pink-and-white sandstone began to chip and collapse.

Then, one massive earthquake eventually destroyed its extraordinary water-supply system.

Unable to rebuild or sustain life any longer, people began to emigrate.

No longer on any trade route, with no worthwhile livelihood to earn and no wealthy visitors from China, Greece or Egypt, Petra was gradually abandoned.

For the next 1,000 years or so, it lay deserted and forgotten – lost to the western world – until our friend Burckhardt rediscovered it in 1812.

Today, Petra – with its stunning sandstone rock cut layout and some 3,000 monuments – is part of the Kingdom of Jordan.

How a city of such stupendous proportions and wonder was created in the middle of the desert, off a mountain rockface, still astonishes the experts.

Where could the Nabataeans have gotten the expertise, the skills and the machinery? they wonder.

Excited tourists from all around the world come to gaze at its striking façade and trample all over its ancient sands.

The Jordanian government has resettled the descendants of Petra's original inhabitants – the Bedouins – near the city.

They have also converted a vast area into a national park.

Now, one of the Seven Wonders of the World and a UNESCO World Heritage Site, Petra has become a popular tourist go-to place – no longer lost or abandoned.

Where is it located: Kingdom of Jordan, 240 km from the capital Amman

Timeframe of Settlement: Fourth century BCE–Seventh century CE

Who discovered it and when: A Swiss silk merchant's son and Arab specialist Johann Ludwig Burckhardt in August 1812. Excavations by international experts, departments and archaeologists are still ongoing.

9

POOMPUHAR

When tsunamis hit...

The Periplus of the Erythraean Sea – an ancient, Greek travelogue from first century CE – referred to it as 'Camara'.

Claudius Ptolemy – a second-century CE Greco-Roman geographer from Egypt – called it 'Khaberis Emporion'.

To the people of the early Chola kingdom, it was known as 'Poompuhar' or 'Kaveripattinam'.

Sitting at the mouth of the 800-km-long Cauvery River where it emptied into the Bay of Bengal, it was an important stop for every ship and boat that sailed by.

It was thus a busy port in ancient Tamil Nadu.

Then, quite surprisingly, it vanished completely from history.

Why did it disappear? How did it disappear?

Was it due to coastal erosion, rising sea levels, a tsunami or a massive cyclone?

It was perhaps all of these and – if legends are to be believed – maybe even a touch of divine wrath.

Poompuhar from all accounts – especially ancient literary texts – was a beautiful town, bustling with life.

Capital of the early Chola kingdom, that existed from 600 BCE–300 CE, it was a thriving trading hub.

It was also their naval base.

Ships from Rome, Egypt, China and Arabia docked and undocked around the clock at the harbour that bordered the shipyard.

Cargo of all kinds, including horses, was loaded, unloaded, checked and stamped with the Chola customs seal – a tiger symbol. Only then were they allowed into the kingdom or sent out, while the rest were stored in granaries and large warehouses abutting the harbour.

It was a prosperous town.

Heaps of precious gems, coral, sandalwood, eaglewood, pearls, gold and other valuable items were sold along its broad, well-laid avenues and marketplaces.

Different merchants, goldsmiths and metalworkers had their own streets – as did butchers and fishmongers, musicians and foreigners.

Citizens lived in terraced mansions with spacious corridors and columns, and their tree-lined gardens – abloom with flowers of every hue – had water-spouting fountains, much like our modern parks.

Foreigners (Greeks were referred to as *Yavanars*) were, however, housed separately in the outskirts.

If you were to take a stroll, you would come across Hindu and Jain temples, along with many prominent Buddhist viharas.

The king was well respected, and everyone looked up to him.

And to ward off evil, for twenty-eight days every year, the town paid homage to Lord Indra – the king of the Devas.

Atop a majestic elephant that lumbered through the streets, a town crier – accompanied by the beat of drums and the blare of trumpets – would proclaim, 'Indra, Lord of the Heavens, is here! Cast out hatred, spread love and joy so that our city may live long, have plentiful rains and our king remains benevolent.'

One year, the king sadly lost his son.

Immersed in grief, he neglected to have Poompuhar celebrate the festival.

This, the people believed, enraged the goddess of Poompuhar.

She perhaps felt that Lord Indra had been slighted.

The sea, according to ancient texts, began to behave strangely.

It receded a few kilometres and then, in one huge dizzying swoop of water – believed to be 400 feet high – gobbled up the whole town.

A town that was teeming with life.

'It is the goddess,' they cried. 'In her fury, she has caused the sea to swallow the whole city.' '*Kadal Kol*' they called it. In Tamil it means 'robbed or destroyed by the sea'.

Just how far this is true is, of course, open to debate.

Later rebuilt over the centuries – some five times over – Poompuhar, as Kaveripattinam, lingered on until about the ninth century, but it perhaps never quite regained the lustre of its heyday.

It was also a gradually decreasing Poompuhar, parts of which were being continually lost to the sea due to soil erosion, constant cyclonic storms, flooding and then being rebuilt or relocated nearby.

Thus, its significance as a vital port also waned.

So, who knows, the wrath of the gods in the form of that first tsunami may well have been the trigger that started the decline.

Finally, Poompuhar – the once-vibrant, two to three-thousand-year-old maritime port of the Cholas – completely vanished from maritime history.

Now, almost 1100 years later, archaeologists, using ancient Tamil texts like *Silappadikaram* and *Manimekalai* – that describe life in Poompuhar – as markers, began searching the seas to see if they could find ancient Poompuhar.

They did.

They found remnants of an ancient town just a few kilometres off the coast in the waters of the Bay of Bengal.

Marine archaeologists also found evidence of a huge tsunami having struck Poompuhar and submerging it completely around third century BCE when the *Kadal Kol* was supposed to have happened.

Excavations nearby, in the villages of Manigramam and Kilayur, revealed a wharf, a brick wall, ring wells, a boat jetty, some Roman coins and remnants of a Buddhist vihara – all dating back to that period – between third century BCE and second century CE.

Furthermore, an unearthed terracotta fragment bearing the imprint of two feet has been hailed as Buddha's *pada*, or feet as well. Poompuhar was once a Buddhist centre, wasn't it?

Underwater excavations by trained diver-archaeologists brought to light a circular, three-course stone structure.

A human-made structure, it was a part of an ancient lighthouse, they happily declared.

Remotely operated vehicles (ROVs) from the National Institute of Ocean Technology (NIOT) also detected multiple construction levels and ancient structures at depths of 50–80 m beneath the seabed.

A layout of an ancient harbour was also discovered, bearing striking similarities to harbour structures found in ancient Egypt, Greece and Rome.

However, before long, disaster struck again.

On 26 December 2004, the sea rose over Poompuhar again.

At about 8 a.m. local time, an undersea earthquake with a magnitude of 9.1 struck off the coast of Indonesia's Sumatra Island.

Within fifteen minutes, tidal waves began slamming into other parts of Indonesia and, in no less than two hours, they had reached Thailand, Sri Lanka and India.

Enormous 30-foot-high waves surged inland, engulfing entire beaches crowded with holidaying tourists and locals.

More than 2,00,000 people across nearly a dozen countries died that day.

In Poompuhar alone, about 170 lives were lost.

Had people not fled for their lives, as they did upon seeing this massive wall of water bearing down upon them, the toll would have been far higher.

Was history perhaps repeating itself?

Today all that remains of the once-flourishing port town are fading memories of hand-me-down tales of ancient maritime glory, a few damaged temples and a sleepy village of about 2,000 fishing families living in constant fear – what if the ocean were to come bearing down upon them once again?

The rest of ancient Poompuhar continues to rest among the fish, lost to the world.

This, then, is the story of the once-fabled Poompuhar that even now continues to intrigue archaeologists who are determined to recover it.

Where is it located: Mayiladuthurai district, Tamil Nadu

Timeframe of Settlement: 600 BCE–300 CE

Who discovered it and when: ASI sponsored excavations began in 1990

10

HAMPI

When wars brutally destroy...

Here's a riddle – can you guess the name of this city or kingdom?

I was once the grand capital of a vast and powerful kingdom.
I was near where Hanuman, the monkey god, used to reside.
I was near where Lord Rama came for help.
My kingdom was known as the city of victory.
I am now in ruins, abandoned and forgotten.
Which city or kingdom am I?

Let's first take the sentences *near where Hanuman used to reside* and *near where Lord Rama came for help.*

Didn't Hanuman, the monkey god, live in a kingdom called Kishkindha?

The epic, Ramayana, tells us he did.

So, if we believe the story of Rama, Kishkindha it must be.

A peak still exists there, named Anjanadri after his place of birth.

Next, where did Rama go for help?

To help rescue Sita, the Ramayana tells us, he went to Sugriva.

And who was Sugriva?

Sugriva was the king of Kishkindha, the monkey kingdom.

Therefore, Rama went to Kishkindha for help.

So, whichever place it was, it was near Kishkindha.

Now the line *my kingdom was known as the city of victory*.

City of victory translates into Vijayanagara, doesn't it?

Thus, it can only mean one place.

Yes, if you've guessed it, then you will know the *city of victory* is the ancient kingdom of Vijayanagara, which means just that – Victory City.

And its once *grand capital* could then only be Hampi, the city of architectural wonders.

Hampi, which is now lying in ruins, *abandoned and forgotten*.

Both Kishkindha and Hampi were a part of a large powerful empire – the famous Vijayanagara Empire, in the southern part of India – now spread over Andhra Pradesh, Telangana and Karnataka.

In fact, Kishkindha and Hampi, legends say, could even be one and the same, so close to each other were they – so that explains the '*near where*', doesn't it?

So, the city of Hampi it is, in the Kingdom of Vijayanagara.

Riddle solved.

Now, how did Hampi come to be in ruins, lost and abandoned?

It all started in the sixteenth century with the military policy followed by Vijayanagara's powerful de facto ruler Aliya Rama Raya who ruled on behalf of Sadashiva Raya, the last proper emperor of the Vijayanagara Empire, an empire that was born in 1336 CE.

Founded by two brothers, Harihara and Bukka, Vijayanagara, by the time Rama Raya took over, had grown to be one of the largest, wealthiest and most powerful kingdoms in southern India.

Unable to live peacefully with his constantly warring Muslim neighbours, Rama Raya began meddling in their affairs.

He started playing one Muslim state against another.

So, the Muslim rulers of Bidar, Bijapur, Ahmednagar, Golconda and Berar – the Muslim Sultanates – got together and decided they'd had enough.

They went to war against him and his powerful Vijayanagara Kingdom and, in the famous battle of Talikota in 1565 CE, defeated him.

Not only did they defeat Vijayanagara, but with pickaxes and crowbars, they viciously hacked and destroyed every beautiful, exquisitely carved temple, statue and pillar they could find.

They wreaked such havoc that when they were done, there was not a single building or sculpture left standing.

The brunt of the carnage was borne by Hampi, its capital.

Why was that?

The city was a symbol of the vast power and wealth of Vijayanagara.

It was on the banks of the River Tungabhadra, a sprawling, booming town surrounded by massive boulders and rocks – boulders and rocks that its kings had made good use of.

They had turned them into brilliantly carved pillars, statues, palaces and temples.

With images, reliefs and frescoes of gods and goddesses and scenes from Indian mythology, these marvellous pieces of architecture were everywhere.

On the banks of the river, in the valleys, among the rocks and on hill tops.

They showcased Hampi's splendour and importance.

As Vijayanagara, the kingdom, had grown in stature, so had Hampi.

So, in the battle of Talikota, they cruelly beheaded Aliya Rama Raya, destroyed his palace, then looted, pillaged and plundered everything in sight.

It was a kind of mindless brutality never seen before.

Thus, a capital city – once teeming with wealthy people and bustling with prosperous traders and eminent scholars; a capital that had some of the world's most stunning architectural wonders; a capital that had been the heart of the Vijayanagara Empire for almost two hundred years – was laid to waste, burnt, wrecked and completely ruined.

Magnificent Hampi, then slowly crumbled, decayed and slipped into neglect and oblivion.

Sadly, Vijayanagara wouldn't have been defeated and sacked but for two of Rama Raya's traitorous generals who had switched sides.

Hampi was thus demolished, but the Empire lingered on under Rama Raya's brother Thirumala Raya, who, with Sadashiva Raya and 550 elephants loaded with treasure, escaped to nearby Penukonda to live another day.

Abandoned by its people, its splendour destroyed forever, Hampi, the once-vibrant capital, however, never quite recovered.

Broken and forgotten, it lay sadly among its own smashed ruins for the next few centuries.

Then, in 1799, a Scottish engineer and antiquarian – a person who collects relics – Colonel Colin Mackenzie, who was to become the first surveyor general of India, hearing rumours of a ruined city, went looking for it.

He found it, drew the first ever survey map of the ruins and produced several watercolour paintings of the monuments.

So, if you want to see his pencil-sketch map of Hampi, you will find it in the British Museum in London.

Also, the first ever photographs of Hampi were taken in 1856 by another colonel in the British army, Alexander Greenlaw.

Then along came Robert Sewell, the British Collector of Bellary, a town in present-day Karnataka.

In 1900, he wrote a book, *A Forgotten Empire: Vijayanagar*. An academic bestseller, it caused a flurry of interest.

It also galvanized the Archaelogical Survey of India into action.

They began improving the site and putting up signs.

Remnants of more than 1,600 monuments, spread over 250 sq. km were excavated, dusted and examined.

Among them was the stone chariot at the Vittala temple, with its wooden finish and minute details.

You might even want to take a ride in it – it looks so ready to roll.

Then there is the Virupaksha temple – still famous and active, which is dedicated to Shiva

“ *Garuda stone chariot at the Vittala temple* ”

And a not-to-miss stone stable for elephants – it is simply astounding.

Although Hampi lies in ruins, the marvellous skill of our ancient sculptors and builders still shines through.

Its cluster of monuments, each more sadly beautiful than the other, is now a tourist wonder.

A UNESCO World Heritage Site, the legacy of a devastated Hampi continues to amaze everyone.

Where is it located: 13 km from Hospet town, Vijayanagara district, Karnataka
Timeframe of Settlement: 1336 CE–1565 CE
Who found it and when: Colonel Colin Mackenzie in 1800. Archaeological Survey of India began work in 1920s.

11

MAMALLAPURAM

When the seas recede...

Once upon a time, off the Tamil Nadu coast in India, flourished a wealthy seaport.

It was called Mamallapuram.

To the seamen of Europe, however, it was known as the prosperous 'Land of the Seven Pagodas'.

How do we know that?

You see, as early as the thirteenth century, Marco Polo, the famous Italian who travelled around the world, identified Mamallapuram as the beautiful port of seven shining *pagoda*s, a tiered towered temple.

So did the Jewish cartographer, Abraham Cresques, in his gold-and-silver paged medieval *Catalan Atlas*.

He called it *Setemelti*, Italian for seven *pagoda*s.

Then there were those countless ancient Tamil texts between the fifth and the ninth centuries that repeatedly mentioned and sang the praises of a prosperous port city Perumpanarruppatai or Kadamallai, with its harbour – Nirppeyarru, off the coast of present-day Tamil Nadu, that identified with Mamallapuram.

So, for that matter, did the seventh-century Chinese traveller H'tsang, who spoke highly of its prosperity.

However, the port was famous, and its praises had been sung long before this as well.

Periplus of the Erythraean Sea – the travel diary of the first-century Greek traveller – spoke of Sopatma, a flourishing seaport north of the river Kaveri.

'Yes,' agreed Ptolemy, a second-century Greek geographer, 'it was a prosperous port,' but he called the port Malange.

Now, it was a city that was also called Mahabalipuram, named after the good King Mahabali of Hindu mythology, who may have ruled there in ancient times and who, having incurred the envy of the devas, was relegated to *Paatal* to fulfil Lord Vishnu's demand for three paces of land.

Or was it named after the great Asura and Vishnu devotee, King Prahalad's grandson, Bali?

One doesn't know, but yes, all without exception however, described the port as a fabulously wealthy and booming trade hub.

So glorious was its reputation that it could even, say Hindu legends, incur the anger and jealousy of Indra, lord of the devas, who may have even wished a flood upon it.

It was really however a port that eventually came to be famously known by the name of its brave seventh-century Pallava king, Mamalla Narsimhavarman I.

Mamalla, meaning wrestler, a king renowned for his warrior skills and valour, who reigned in 642 CE, and who also built architectural wonders to the gods on the shores of the Bay of Bengal – especially after his victory over a powerful Chalukyan king.

And so, it became the wondrous land of the great warrior, Mamalla.

Thus, a port city with many names and a singularly marvellous reputation – that was Mamallapuram.

Yet, despite such legendary references and numerous descriptions, no one for thousands of years had seen hide or hair of this astounding city or its seven gold-covered *pagoda*s.

Apart from a rock-cut shore temple plus some *rathas* or chariots, five of which were in honour of the Mahabharata's Pandava brothers and their wife, Draupadi – along with a sculpted rockface granite piece known as 'Arjuna's Penance' or 'Descent of the Ganges', a few cave temples, an elephant and a bull sculpture – no other evidence lay around on land or underwater to tell us that a wonderful, bustling port such as the land of the seven shining *pagoda*s, had truly existed – unless the shore temple was one of Marco Polo's famous *pagoda*s – which they now say it is – but then, where was the shine?

Thus, Mamallapuram or Mahabalipuram, considering its fabulous reputation, was a 'lost' city in the true sense of the word.

So, if it existed at all, its fame as the prosperous land of the seven shining *pagoda*s must be a part of ancient South Indian lore or mythology – or so everyone believed.

Otherwise, how could a port city of such grandeur so completely disappear?

However, a few years ago, that particular theory went for a super toss.

'Why?' you might ask.

On 26 December 2004, at about 8 a.m. local time, an undersea earthquake with a magnitude of 9.1 on the Richter scale struck the Indonesian island of Sumatra.

In no less than two hours, huge tidal waves reached Sri Lanka and India.

The massive tsunami that hit Poompuhar ravaged the coast at Mahabalipuram as well.

As fishermen ran for their lives, they saw a strange sight.

They saw the sea recede or pull back at least 500 m before it came rushing back at them.

At that precise moment, they caught a glimpse of several huge ghost-like, rock-cut structures rising out of the seabed before the sea swallowed them up again.

It was an eerie sight.

One that has stayed with the survivors.

Luckily, unlike Poompuhar, there were no casualties.

As soon as the storm abated, the National Institute of Oceanography (NIO) and the Navy got to work.

Divers were sent in, and sonar booms were deployed underwater.

A temple wall, some 6 feet high and 230 feet long, was discovered.

Many rock-cut structures and blocks were found.

On the shore, thanks to the tsunami, several other ancient artefacts – some regal sculptures of peacocks, horses, a lion and even an unfinished stone elephant – popped up.

As the experts went deeper, they were thrilled to find more and more proof of an even larger settlement – probably from the seventh century.

Once again, like Dwarka, myth had turned into reality.

The impact of the receding sea had knocked off 6–7 feet of sand that had covered these structures.

Thousands and thousands of tons of sand had shifted or moved, exposing what lay under.

Now, before the 2004 tsunami, in 2001–2002, marine archaeologists from NIO – referring to ancient texts – had already begun excavations.

Carbon dating of underwater relics at the time had indicated massive floodings in two phases around the same area.

They had concluded that there had been one submersion in the first century and another in the fourteenth century.

In 2001–2002 members of the Scientific Exploration Society from the UK had also scoped the waters.

However, now the ocean itself had – with this new tsunami – made it easier for these experts.

If the excavated granite remnants are proof, they have no doubt that the other six rock-cut *pagoda*s or temples are likely embedded deep in the seabed.

Thus, Mamallapuram was no mythical city, nor were its seven *pagodas* a fable.

The lonely shore temple was definitely one of the sparkling *pagodas*, they believe.

Innumerable ancient Roman coins and rock cave inscriptions bearing dates and names of Pallava personalities have also been found.

Proof again of a once-glorious, thriving port city in a kingdom where kings ruled wisely, people were happy and trade, art, literature and architecture – rock-cut – flourished.

UNESCO, in 1984, tagged this seventh- to eighth-century group of monuments as a World Heritage Site.

Today, attempts are being made to raise the vast sunken city that still lies mysteriously deep and lost within the ocean.

In the meanwhile, tourists from across the world gaze with wonder and eyes anew at the onshore remains of the city once called Mamallapuram – now Mahabalipuram.

Where is it located: Off the Bay of Bengal, 60 km from Chennai

Timeframe of Settlement: First century CE or earlier – Fourteenth century CE

Who discovered it and when: National Institute of Oceanography between 2001–2017

12

ANGKOR

When empires crumble...

Here's an open secret: Angkor was never lost.

However, if you google 'lost cities', Angkor will be one of the first to pop up.

Neglected? Yes.

Deserted? Perhaps.

But lost or forgotten? Not quite.

Angkor was the capital of the once-mighty Khmer empire known as Kambuja – an empire in Indochina (a region in Southeast Asia) that is today known as Cambodia.

With its collection of huge Hindu temples and architectural wonders, it was the seat of its *Deva-rajas,* or 'God-kings'.

Its Hindu rulers believed they were divine and so ruled over a state that replicated Heaven on Earth.

High on Angkor's Phnom Bakheng hill, built to replicate Mount Meru, the abode of the gods, is a conical temple dedicated to Lord Shiva, whom they believed they themselves represented.

It was encircled by water-filled moats, reservoirs, waterways and canals that imitated the oceans that surrounded Meru.

Sometime in the ninth century, Khmer King Jayavarman II of Kambuja united all the little principalities around him to form one big, prosperous and powerful Khmer empire.

Then, later in the same century, Yasovarman I set about turning Angkor, its capital, into a sacred landscape.

His successor, Suryavarman II, not to be found lagging, crowned it between the years 1113 CE and 1150 CE with one of the most massive and spectacular Hindu temple complexes ever built.

And it was… you guessed it: *Angkor Wat* – meaning, 'city of temples'.

Adorned with hundreds of statues of *apsaras* and *devas*, Angkor Wat was absolutely stupendous.

Its walls, lined with exquisitely carved reliefs of scenes from the Mahabharata and the Ramayana, stretched for hundreds of yards.

It depicted mythical events and characters, such as the Kurma or tortoise avatar – the second of Lord Vishnu's ten avatars or incarnations, which he took on to save the world, and the churning of the ocean of milk by the devas and the asuras to obtain the elixir of life, from the Hindu religious text Vishnu Purana.

And along with, yes, Suryavarman holding court (which was not mythical).

Its five fir-cone towers represented Meru's five peaks.

Then came Jayavarman VII.

He built several more magnificent temples and beautified Angkor even further.

However, he converted to Buddhism, and all the Khmer temples turned into Buddhist shrines.

Buddhism replaced Hinduism as the state religion.

Jayavarman VII then built the magnificent Buddhist temple of Bayon, with sculptures of gigantic human faces that were said to represent him as an avatar of Buddha.

"A bronze replica of one of the twenty-three stone images of King Jayavarman VII sent to different parts of the kingdom in 1191"

The grandeur of Hinduism was thus beginning to be replaced by Buddhism's monk sobriety.

Right up to the sixteenth century its successive kings continued to reign and build, but perhaps, with not quite as much as much zeal as their predecessors.

Interestingly, all the temples were in stone while the people lived in wooden houses.

Throughout their reign, the Khmer kings, however, had to contend with warring neighbours – and it had begun to take its toll.

So, in the fifteenth century, when Angkor's neighbour, Siam – present-day Thailand – mounted a brutal attack on Angkor, it more or less ended the Khmer reign.

Tired of the hard work of converting Angkor into a sacred place, its king perhaps had no energy or enthusiasm left to take a firm military stand.

The Khmer king, along with his followers, fled to a new city – Phnom Penh, which is Cambodia's capital today – leaving all the architectural wonders they had helped build to nature.

And all this while, a gradual climatic change had begun as well.

Heavy monsoons often flooded and damaged the city.

Drought would then set in, and there would be no water in Angkor, causing its marvellous and complicated irrigation systems to fail.

Angkor was thus no longer the booming city it once was.

Gradually, the city fell into disrepair and neglect

A jungle sprang up – trees, bushes and vines – and took over the city.

The foliage spread rampantly and swallowed whole walls and entire buildings.

Over time, with the weight of the overgrowth, the city's spectacular temples, roads and canals crumbled and disappeared beneath the encroaching vegetation.

However, the faithful people who still lived nearby continued to light a candle to the past.

At this point in time, in mid-nineteenth century CE, Henri Mouhot, a French naturalist and explorer, arrived in Cambodia.

He travelled around, and while some say he stumbled upon it while following a butterfly or some other insect, others say a Christian padre led him to Angkor's hidden temples.

Mouhot was amazed to find a fabulous city-complex spread over some 250 km with seventy-two huge temples and hundreds of smaller ones.

'Grander than anything left to us by Greece or Rome,' he said, stunned at the vast scale and grandeur of Angkor.

Four times the size of the Vatican – the Catholic holy city – the Angkor Wat temple's archaeological complex itself covered something like 400 acres.

Excited, he proclaimed to the world that he had discovered, 'an amazing lost city, the lost city of Angkor!'

Now, at the time, France, as a colonial power in South-East Asia, was in the process of acquiring Cambodia as a French protectorate.

Henri Mouhot being a proud Frenchman who came from what he probably believed was a more advanced civilization, felt that he had discovered a city that was fantastic but lost in the wilderness.

Mouhot's findings were published by the *Royal Geographical Society* and, as usual, they caused a sensation in Europe.

They became euphoric over a lost-but-found city in Cambodia.

Strangely, it didn't strike them that anything so spectacular, that had existed for thousands of years, was not necessarily 'lost' just because they were unaware of it or had only just discovered it.

Nevertheless, to this day, Angkor is on the list of lost cities they rediscovered.

However, why it was built on such a large scale only to be abandoned centuries later still foxes the experts.

French archaeologists soon began meticulously restoring Angkor's remarkable monuments.

Later, many other countries including India joined in.

Aerial mapping was done.

It was even scanned by radar from the U.S. space shuttle Endeavour, and Angkor's grandeur and spread stunned the world.

How they managed to create such a massive and intricately carved stone complex with no modern equipment is something that still mystifies us.

Now a UNESCO World Heritage Site and partially restored, Angkor – a victim of the Western myth of the lost-city theory – is now happily basking in its newfound glory.

Where is it located: Northwest Cambodia, near present-day Siem Reap

When was it founded: Ninth century CE–Seventeenth century CE

Who discovered it and when: French explorer Henri Mouhot in nineteenth century CE

13

NALANDA

When invaders destroy...

Xuanzang was one of China's greatest scholars.

He lived in the seventh century and was an avid traveller too.

On the road for almost sixteen-odd years, travelling through Central Asia and India, he visited various Buddhist centres of learning.

Then, when he decided it was time to return home, he did so – with twenty horse-loads of some 520 boxes of manuscripts he hoped to translate.

And you will never guess where the bulk of his manuscripts came from.

Be prepared to be surprised.

They were from Nalanda Mahavihara, a university town whose ruins lie near Rajgir, in present-day Bihar.

Nalanda Mahavihara was a residential university – apparently, the world's *first*.

The famous Oxford of Britain hadn't been born yet, nor had Cambridge.

With 10,000 student-monks, 1,500 teachers and an elaborate lecture-cum-residential complex, the world's best students and scholars wrote, argued, discussed and debated every subject under the sun there.

From Buddhism and its immense cache of scriptural literature to mathematics, medicine, religion, geography, logic, philosophy, science, Ayurveda, grammar, astronomy, you name it, Nalanda taught them all.

Amazed by the scale of academics at Nalanda, Xuanzang spent about two years there.

Then, when he got home, he wrote about it in his travelogue, *The Great Tang Records of the Western Regions*.

And in their own travelogues, so did fellow Chinese travellers Yijing – who later stayed for ten years – and H'tsang, who spent five years there.

And that is how we know so much about the greatness of Nalanda.

Thus, with students and faculty from China, Korea, Japan, Tibet, Mongolia and Sri Lanka, it was a hugely popular postgraduate university.

Now, why was it called Nalanda Mahavihara?

Perhaps because, in Sanskrit, *Na allam-da* meant 'giver of knowledge'. Or it could be because 100 years earlier, 500 merchants had gotten together, and bought and gifted a mango grove to Buddha.

A grove where a *nāga* (snake), known to the locals as Nalanda, lived.

Buddha was known to have preached there, so it was already connected to his teachings.

Hence the name – and the reason for the choice of location.

Nalanda, thus, had many Buddhist luminaries as well.

Nāgārjuna – the Mahayana Buddhist expert known as the second Buddha – taught there, as did our other genius who discovered zero – Āryabhaṭa, who was at one time its principal.

Now Xuanzang tells us that a Śakrāditya (415–455 CE) of the Gupta dynasty founded the university.

Other scholars say that it was King Kumāragupta I of the Gupta dynasty who did, and that Śakrāditya and Kumāragupta are one and the same.

Well, whatever name he was known by, the university he established – and which all his successors happily promoted – went on to flourish for the next 750 years as the world's premier centre of learning.

It had hundreds of classrooms where students were taught, well-laid dormitories where they stayed, and a fabulous nine-storeyed library with at least nine-million books – manuscripts on every conceivable subject.

Handwritten, palm-leaf manuscripts were housed in little niches in alcoves that students were required to check in and check out, as they do today.

It had a very strict admission policy too.

It wasn't easy to get in.

Students had to be twenty years old and were put through rigorous tests that tested their scholastic ability and knowledge before being admitted.

Soon, however, as its fame spread, it attracted unwanted attention.

A thriving centre of Buddhism and learning was like a magnet to bigots and unbelievers.

The first attack came during the reign of Skandagupta.

The Huns – nomads from Central Asia – under Mihirakula, in the latter half of the fifth century, ransacked Nalanda.

Nalanda, however, managed to survive the attack.

King Skandagupta and his successors restored and rehoused it in an even bigger complex.

The second attack was in the seventh century, by the Gaudas – rulers of a medieval kingdom of Bengal – during the reign of Emperor Harshavardhana.

Nalanda withstood this onslaught as well, and Emperor Harsha restored it once again.

Then, towards the end of the twelfth century, came the Turkish leader, Bakhtiyar Khalji.

His was the most brutal and destructive of attacks, one from which Nalanda never recovered.

Although scholars today say this attack couldn't have happened and that Nalanda was destroyed due to other reasons, the general belief is that Bakhtiyar did destroy Nalanda, and it was for one of these three reasons.

One – Bakhtiyar had heard of the greatness of Nalanda, and such was his anger against Buddhism that he wanted to destroy it.

Two – he went in search of a Qur'an that he hoped to find in Nalanda, but when he didn't, he set fire to it in a fit of rage.

Three – Bakhtiyar was seriously unwell, and when he was cured not by an Islamic doctor but by a Nalanda Buddhist monk, he was so enraged that he razed Nalanda to the ground.

Whatever the reason, Nalanda's famous library was reduced to ashes.

Its flames rising high into the sky, the buildings smouldered for many months before finally dying down.

Many scholars were killed. Those who survived were forced to flee, carrying just fistfuls of precious manuscripts.

Nalanda slowly slipped into oblivion – and, buried in its own ashes, lay thus for the next 700 years, lost to the world.

Until one day, in 1812, some locals brought the ruins to the attention of a Scottish surgeon, Francis Buchanan-Hamilton, who was also a geographer, surveyor-cum-botanist and zoologist, credited with setting up the Calcutta Alipore Zoo.

Hamilton checked it out.

A portrait of Alexander Cunningham

He, however, didn't realize the ruins were what was left of Nalanda mounds.

It was Major Markham Kittoe – a British-Bengal infantry officer who was also an explorer and archaeologist – who later made that connection.

Enter the Archaeological Survey of India chief Alexander Cunningham and his men.

They discovered across many buildings, thick layers of ash in the uppermost strata of soil that confirmed destruction by fire.

Stupa mounds, brick remains of eleven monasteries, rows of dormitories and libraries were then gradually uncovered.

Recovered, among countless inscriptions, literary evidence, seals and ruined artworks – some 13,000 in all – was an inscription that supported its restoration and mentioned the destruction by fire of Nalanda's library of manuscripts.

Some relics, when carbon-dated, were found to go back to a period even before Lord Buddha.

So far, only twenty-three hectares of the original sprawling site have been excavated.

Just imagine in the fifth century – almost 500 years before any of the world's great universities came into being – Nalanda, in India, was already a fully functioning centre of learning.

So, inspired by its original monasteries and layout, India and seventeen other countries have come together to rebuild the lost university in Rajgir, Bihar, and restore it to its previous position of repute.

Spread over 485 acres, built at a cost of Rs 1,800 crores, its first batch of students were admitted in 2014.

Where is it located: Near the town of Bihar Sharif, 95 km from Patna

Timeframe of Settlement: Fifth century CE–Thirteenth century CE

Who discovered it and when:
Francis Buchanan-Hamilton in 1812;
Major Markham Kittoe in 1847;
ASI under Sir Alexander Cunningham between 1915–1937

14

MUZIRIS

When beads popped up...

About 25 km from the city of Kochi in Kerala lies Pattanam.

On the surface, nondescript and ordinary, the village of Pattanam was no different from most others in Kerala.

Its only claim to fame – if any – was the famous Periyar River that flowed alongside.

However, all that was about to change…

For below the ground, it was a different story altogether.

A few years ago, it happened to be a season of heavy downpours.

Catching a break, a group of children were playing hopscotch on the banks of the Periyar at Pattanam.

As they hopped, skipped and jumped, they kicked up something curious.

It was a cache of unusual beads and battered coins washed up by the rains.

Strange and different, the beads caused a sensation.

Soon in a matter of months, life altered for the village of Pattanam.

A sleepy Pattanam, otherwise known in Malayalam as *Pashnam*, came awake.

So, how did that happen?

Now, Pattanam is also about 11 km away from the more important town of Kodungalloor.

Kodungalloor – or Cranganore, as it was known during the time of the British, is where the River Periyar meets the Arabian Sea.

It had long been believed to be the site of one of Kerala's legendary and ancient, but now extinct, ports.

Can you guess its name?

Well, 2,000 years ago, it was famously known as Muziris.

Considered the gateway to India, the port was where traders from as far as Rome and Greece, Yemen and Arabia once anchored to peddle their wares.

Creating waves on the Periyar River, they came in beautiful vessels carrying gold, coral, fine crystal, wine and olive oil, and departed with exotic spices and nuts from Kerala.

It was a compulsory port of call where gold and silver were constantly exchanged for thousands of tons of Kerala's 'black gold' – otherwise known to us as pepper.

Thus, Muziris was a popular destination in ancient India for sea traders.

It has been mentioned in several famous old Tamil and Malayalam texts from the first to the fifth century – *Akanaṉūṟu*, *Purananuru* and other Sangam literature.

It was even marked on the world's ancient maritime map – the *Tabula Peutingeriana*, a fifth-century Roman map.

And even described by several famous Greek and Roman travellers like Pliny the Elder and Claudius Ptolemy, who made the journey. In fact, when Pliny the Elder of Rome wrote about Muziris, he referred to it as the world's first emporium.

Interestingly, Muziris was also where St. Thomas, the apostle of Christ, first arrived; where India's first mosque, the Cheraman Juma Masjid, was built; where the Jews first landed and built their synagogues.

And where the Dutch, the Portuguese, the Chinese, the Phoenicians and the Arabs mingled.

So yes, Muziris was an important trading port always buzzing with foreigners and visitors.

Then suddenly, sometime in the fourteenth century, Muziris ceased to exist.

Like Poompuhar and Mamallapuram, it went off the map completely.

Its very name seemed to have been mysteriously lost.

If it had existed at all, it was now nowhere to be found – not on land nor in any later-written accounts of travellers or traders.

It was as if it didn't – or hadn't – existed at all.

Was it all a lie? A myth or a legend handed down from ancient times?

Was there, except in ancient stories, no Muziris at all?

To find out, sporadic excavations were conducted at Kodungalloor between 1945 and 1983.

However, to everyone's disappointment, nothing earlier than thirteenth-century artefacts was recovered.

Then, in 2007, after that fateful rainy day when those children discovered the cache of 2,000 beads and coins, archaeological attention shifted to Pattanam, north of Kodungalloor town.

Excavations were conducted and – lo and behold – what an unbelievable treasure trove Pattanam turned out to be.

An incredible number of artefacts were revealed and recovered.

Some 4.5 million pieces of ancient Indian pottery and 1,41,348 pieces of non-Indian pottery have emerged so far – some even dating back to fifth century BCE.

Among the many broken shards was a tiny, oval-shaped agate band ring with a sphinx from Thebes in Egypt, and a seemingly endless cache of Roman artefacts.

And guess what has delighted the astonished experts most?

The discovery of two 6-metre-long canoes and a large brick wharf with some nine teak bollards or pillars.

Yes – and what's even more surprising is the massive number of artefacts unearthed from just a small area around Pattanam.

Now, even though inscriptions on a Jewish copper plate dated 1000 CE referred to Kodungalloor as Muyirikkode, another name for Muziris, historians and archaeologists are convinced – although there are still some who refute this – that Muyirikkode, or the famous Muziris, or Muchiri, or Muchiripattnam, must have been centred in Pattanam and not Kodungalloor.

Yes, maybe. But for all we know, both the legendary port of Muziris and the village of Pattanam may perhaps have been part of the larger settlement of Kodungalloor. Kodungalloor or Pattanam – does it really matter?

Isn't it enough to know that we now have proof of a famous lost port city that is no longer mere legend or myth?

So, what could've happened to Muziris?

How did Muziris as a port go extinct or get so totally forgotten?

Why had such a legendary port – one that had hosted mariners and sea traders from the Mediterranean, the River Nile, the Red Sea, the Indian Ocean and the South China Sea – suddenly and inexplicably drop off the map?

Had trade with Rome declined, causing Muziris to decline as well?

Nobody knows for sure.

However, all clues point to a massive thunderstorm that occurred around 1341 CE and a tidal wave flooding the Periyar river.

It was a deluge like no other.

It had overrun coastal Kodungalloor and had, perhaps, inundated most of the little hamlets in and around it as well.

It must have swept away, or drowned, the famous Muziris port too.

Then, for the next few hundred years and more, all activity may have ceased – no huge ships crested the waves, no great trade and definitely no gold or pepper came for barter or exchange.

Thus, into oblivion it sank.

Today, as we continue to dig and excavate, who knows – more clues may surface to pinpoint its exact location and tell us what really happened to Muziris.

However, isn't it astonishing that for centuries, Pattanam – such an ordinary and unassuming village – had been hiding a secret so extraordinary within her very folds, below ground?

And it took another intervention by the rain gods for that secret to be revealed.

Could the famous lost Muziris, perhaps, be calling out to be rediscovered?

Where is it located: In Kerala, India, about 35 km from the town of Kochi

Timeframe of Settlement: First century CE– Fourteenth century CE

Who discovered it and when:

ASI–Muziris Heritage Project 2007 -still ongoing

15

XANADU

When a lost city becomes an inspiration...

A famous English poem. A popular Broadway hit song. A region around planet Saturn. And a legendary town in Mongolia.

What would they have in common?

Nothing, you might say. However, they do.

And here's a clue: they share the same name.

Not too difficult, was it?

No?

Well, the name is 'Xanadu'.

And it is the name of the legendary capital of a vast Mongolian empire.

So, what is so special about Xanadu that it should be so famous and popular?

Xanadu was known for its great warrior kings, fabulous palaces and lavish lifestyle.

And over the centuries it came to mean an exotic and luxurious place that was mysterious to boot, because as early as the thirteenth century the Italian explorer Marco Polo triggered off this image of Xanadu as a city of fascinating grandeur.

“*A mosaic of Marco Polo*”

As a seventeen-year-old, he had set out from Venice to explore the world.

He covered 24,000 km in twenty-four years, seventeen of which he spent in China's Mongolian empire.

Writing about his stay between 1275 CE and 1292 CE at Xanadu in his *The Travels of Marco Polo* he made Xanadu sound magical, almost like a place of fantasy.

He described Xanadu and the ruler's exquisite marble palace with its golden rooms adorned with paintings and sculptures of people, animals, birds and flowers as…

> *The halls and chambers are all gilt, and very handsome... In the centre of these grounds, where there is a beautiful grove of trees, he has built a royal pavilion, supported upon a colonnade of handsome pillars, gilt and varnished...*

And the image of Xanadu as a fabulous place probably took off from there.

Then S.T. Coleridge, the celebrated eighteenth-century British poet, made Xanadu even more famous with his poem 'Kubla Khan', which was all about the great Kublai Khan, ruler of – no guesses – fabulous Xanadu. He tells us that:

In Xanadu did Kubla Khan
A stately pleasure-dome decree:
Where Alph, the sacred river, ran...
And there were gardens bright with sinuous rills,
Where blossomed many an incense-bearing tree;
And here were forests ancient as the hills...

So, no doubt taking a cue from all that, Australian pop singer Olivia Newton-John's title song from the Broadway 1980 musical 'Xanadu' was about a love that could possibly come true only in an idyllic place called Xanadu, as she sang:

A place where nobody dared to go,
The love that we came to know...
They call it Xanadu (it takes your breath and it'll leave you blind)...
We're in Xanadu (you dream of it, we offer you)...
A million lights are dancing and there you are, a shooting star...
An everlasting world... Xanadu, Xanadu...

It was such a hit it's popular to this day.

It also helped to spread Xanadu's reputation as an enchanting place – a mysteriously beautiful place lost to the world.

As for the planet Saturn, US-based NASA – apparently inspired by Coleridge's poem – decided to name a highly reflective and radar-bright area on the leading hemisphere of Saturn's largest moon, Titan – yes, Xanadu.

Its striking terrain may have appeared similar to Earth's beautiful flowing rivers, mountains and sand dunes, and probably seemed like fairyland to them.

So, need we say more?

Xanadu, from all accounts, was among the most fantastic ancient cities of lost splendour one had ever heard of.

Thus, today, 700 years later, it remains one among the many cities lost but perhaps not completely forgotten – thanks to its inspiring nature.

The great Chengiz Khan of Mongolia, notorious for his ruthlessness and cruelty, was, however, also a military genius.

Thus, his grand empire covered most of Asia and stretched right up to Europe.

After his time, his empire was ruled by his descendants, one of whom was his grandson, the famous Kublai Khan, the founder of the Yuan dynasty.

Xanadu – otherwise known as Shangdu – was Kublai Khan's capital.

Designed according to feng shui rules in 1256 by Liu Bingzhong, Kublai Khan's Chinese advisor, it was a magnificent walled city, with grand palaces, huge statues and eye-catching buildings.

It was also blessed with, again in the words of Marco Polo:

> *... beautiful meadows, watered by many rivulets, where a variety of animals of the deer and goat kind were pastured.*

However, Kublai Khan soon built Beijing nearby and turned that into his main capital, only moving to the cool climes of Xanadu every summer.

So, for much of the fourteenth century, Xanadu, in the northwest of China, became just the summer capital of the Yuan dynasty.

A vibrantly glorious Xanadu thus began to slowly lose its importance.

Then, with the rise of the Ming dynasty in China, the Yuan dynasty fell.

Fabulous Xanadu was then sacked and destroyed by the Ming.

Its buildings plundered and brutally pillaged, it became a shadow of its previous self.

With the power centre shifting elsewhere, to Beijing, Xanadu gradually fell into complete disrepair.

It lay, thus, among its ruins – mysteriously distant and considered lost by the world.

All we have today are some stone ruins of a once beautiful city that boasted of a splendid 'pleasure dome' of a palace of marble and gilt.

However, its reputation and fame as an exotic place never really died and continues to be extolled to this day.

Now a UNESCO World Heritage Site, humungous stone carvings of Kublai Khan alongside a few others will welcome you at the fenced and clearly marked site.

They mark the thirty-four-year rule of the legendary ruler, and the hundred-year reign of the Yuan dynasty.

Come summer, the grasslands that hosted the once famous capital become a breathtaking carpet of golden nasturtiums.

Sadly, however, the sporadically crumbling remnants of Xanadu's once-magnificent palaces, temples, tombs, nomadic camps and waterways appear to be visibly lost – in a place where visitors are rare and nature has taken its toll.

Even so, the lost splendour of Xanadu continues to inspire.

Where is it located: 350 km from China's present capital, Beijing, Inner Mongolia autonomous region

Timeframe of Settlement: 1256 CE–1430 CE

Who discovered it and when: The archaeological department of the People's Republic of China in the nineteenth century.

16

DHANUSHKODI

When cyclones make land fall...

On 17 December 1964, a deep tropical depression formed over the South Andaman Sea in the Bay of Bengal.

By 19 December, it had intensified into a furious cyclonic storm.

On 20 December, accompanied by massive thunderstorms, it began moving westwards towards Sri Lanka.

On 21 December, gobbling up 400 to 500 km per day at speeds ranging between 150 and 200 mph, it crossed Vavuniya in Sri Lanka.

At midnight on 22 December, it hurtled into India.

Then, with 170 mph winds and twenty-foot-high waves, it made a devastating landfall at Dhanushkodi.

Dhanushkodi, a 10-km-strip of a town at the tip of the island of Rameswaram – or Pamban Island, as it is otherwise known – lies off the coast of Tamil Nadu, India.

And a flourishing, thriving Dhanushkodi, once buzzing with life, was no more.

At just about that time, some 30 km away, a little before midnight, the Pamban-Dhanushkodi passenger train number 653, also known as the Boat Mail, had pulled out of Pamban station.

Leaving the town of Pamban, which was the first point of halt on the island of Rameswaram from mainland India, it was on its way to Dhanushkodi with about 200 passengers.

Halfway through, the downpour intensified.

"Remains of Dhanushkodi railway station"

The driver may have tried to signal the Dhanushkodi station.

However, the signals were down.

He halted for about an hour, and being neither here nor there, and between stations, he decided to cautiously forge ahead.

And that was the last time he – or anybody else on Train 653 – went anywhere.

As the cyclone in all its fury made landfall in Dhanushkodi the seawaters rose as one.

Tidal waves, 20-25 feet high, engulfed the entire town, rushed inwards to meet the train, ripped off its engine and dragged the six coaches – filled with sleeping passengers – into the sea.

But that was not all.

The 2-km-long Pamban Bridge – which connected mainland Tamil Nadu, stretching from the town of Mandapam to Rameswaram and Dhanushkodi at Pamban – was also completely washed away.

Only its piers were left standing, looking lost and forlorn.

While hurricane gales lashed Mandapam, the town of Pamban and the rest of Rameswaram barely survived.

With most of Dhanushkodi submerged under the sea, other than the stone walls built by the British, nothing remained.

Thus, overnight, in the blink of an eye, hundreds of lives were lost, Rameswaram was cut off from mainland India and Dhanushkodi destroyed.

While news of the cyclone and the Pamban Bridge going underwater was flashed across the nation, no one knew until the next day that the train had also been devoured by the rampaging waves.

It was only when someone saw the chimney of the train engine protruding from the water almost thirty-six hours later that the train and its sad fate were known.

Two railway men patrolling the Pamban railway bridge clung to the frame of the bridge for several hours before they were rescued.

Killing scores of residents and stranding thousands, the terrible cyclone left in its wake such massive destruction that the town of Dhanushkodi was lost forever.

Are you wondering what Danushkodi was like before it was destroyed?

Well, Dhanushkodi had been a popular little town – a serene beach town famous for its natural beauty and legendary status.

It lay 30 km away from Pamban town and 18 km away from Rameswaram town, surrounded by the sea at the tip of the Rameswaram Island, facing Sri Lanka.

Thus, it was also just 30 km away from Talaimannar in Sri Lanka and had been, since the days of the British, a crucial link connecting Sri Lanka and India.

With temples, hospitals, a church, a post office and some schools, it had been a cosmopolitan trade-cum-pilgrim hub where the two countries had met for years.

Boats had regularly plied, ferrying people and goods to and fro since the early 1900s – especially after the Pamban bridge had been built in 1914.

It was also said to be deeply connected to the story of Rama – The Ramayana.

Dhanushkodi was where the hero of the epic, Rama, and his army of bears, elephants and monkeys – the *vanar sena* – built the Ram Setu, which enabled them to cross over and rescue Sita from Ravana's clutches.

The string of limestone shoals between Dhanushkodi and Sri Lanka – still visible in certain spots under the sea and even detected by NASA – is believed to be that very bridge.

Dhanushkodi was also where Rama, with his *dhanush* (or bow), had supposedly crowned Ravana's brother Vibhishana as the king of Lanka after killing Ravana.

Upon Vibhishana's insistence, Rama had also ended – or destroyed – *kodi*, the Ram Setu, after crossing back to India.

"A 20th century painting of vanaras building bridge to Lanka"

Hence the names *Dhanushkodi* and *Rameswaram* – land of Rama.

If we need any more confirmation that this was Rama's land, all we have to do is check out the Kothandaramar temple.

Dedicated to Rama, Lakshmana, Sita, Hanuman and Vibhishana, Kothandaramar temple still stands between Dhanushkodi and Rameswaram town.

Ancient though it is, the temple appears to have amazingly survived the cyclone.

Now, in Rameswaram town itself is the impressive Ramanathaswamy Temple.

With a name like that, you would expect it to be dedicated to Lord Rama, wouldn't you?

Nope. Strangely enough, it's a Shiva temple – and an important one at that.

It is where Rama is supposed to have prayed to Lord Shiva, seeking forgiveness for killing Ravana, a devotee of Lord Shiva.

And that is why pilgrims, not just traders, flock to Rameswaram and Dhanushkodi.

Both are so entwined with the story of Rama that now, with Dhanushkodi gone and Rameswaram left bereft, it feels like a piece of India's ancient history is lost.

Although the Pamban Road Bridge between Mandapam and Rameswaram Island was rebuilt within six months, the railway lines are gone and the part of Rameswaram that boasted of Dhanushkodi is now a wasteland.

Dhanushkodi, or what is left of it today, is a ghost town where ruins litter the beach.

Apart from a few fishing families, it is uninhabited.

Shrubs and casuarina trees dot the white sands, with puddles of water in between.

Arichal Munai, or the last point, about 5 km out, is where the blue choppy waters of the Bay of Bengal meet the relatively calm green of the Indian Ocean.

On a clear day you can easily see Sri Lanka from there.

All is now blissfully calm and peaceful on the island of Rameswaram – that is, until maybe the next cyclone strikes.

Where is it located: Off the east coast of Tamil Nadu, on the island of Rameswaram
Timeframe of Settlement: Seventh century BCE–1964 CE
Who discovered it and when: It was abandoned

17

NAGARJUNAKONDA

When progress destroys history...

Mr Suraparaju Venkataramayya was intrigued.

Grazing their cattle in the forests of Pullareddygudem, in the valley of Nagarjunakonda nearby, some villagers had discovered a few old structures and mounds.

He decided to go and check them out.

And what he saw among the overgrown thorny bushes stunned him.

Peeping out through the foliage, were some enormous, exquisitely carved and inscribed ancient stone pillars.

He couldn't read the script, but he knew it had to be something significant.

'There must have been an ancient settlement here,' he muttered to himself. 'I am but a local schoolteacher. What do I know? I need to bring in the experts.'

So off he went to inform the Archaeological Survey of India.

The ASI swung into action and, to his delight, confirmed that it was an important archaeological site indeed.

Located 250 km from Hyderabad in Andhra Pradesh on the banks of the river Krishna, it was one of the most significant finds of British India.

Excitement ran high as ruins of several Buddhist monasteries, stupas, Buddha statues, sculptures and monuments were excavated.

Most impressive among them was the 80-foot-high, 100-foot-wide Great Stupa.

When the ruins of a university and a monastery of the third and fourth century CE were found, it established beyond doubt that this was where the famous Mahayana Nagarjuna, a key Buddhist philosopher, had lived and lectured.

Over a hundred other inscriptions, reliefs, antiques and temples dating back to 278 CE and first century CE, as well as those of kings and queens of the Ikshvaku dynasty, were also discovered.

They not only told us that Buddhism had flourished in what was then known as the city of Vijayapuri – the capital of the rich and prosperous Ikshvaku Kingdom – but that Vijayapuri had been an important centre of Buddhist learning where great minds from across South-

East Asia had met and from where Buddhism probably spread to the rest of the world.

Vijayapuri then – somewhere along the way, perhaps thanks to the monastery that was named after Nagarjuna – became Nagarjunakonda.

As some beautiful temple-remains have also been unearthed, Hinduism too must have existed side by side.

Vijayapuri, a well-planned city, even boasted of a unique amphitheatre that could have easily seated a 1,000 people.

However, that was not all.

Further excavations produced even more startling and astonishing finds.

Apart from some Stone Age tools, Roman coins of emperors – Tiberius, dated between 16 to 37 CE, along with those of Antoninus Pius and his wife Faustina the Elder from 141 CE – emerged.

What do they tell us?

Firstly, Vijayapuri had been around for a very long time indeed, maybe about 5,000 years, since the Stone Age goes back that far.

Secondly, there existed trade relations between the Telugus of Andhra Pradesh and ancient Rome even as early as the first or second century CE.

Equally interesting was the discovery of a relief of some Scythian soldiers wearing caps and coats and a lightly bearded, semi-nude man carrying a drinking horn, with a barrel of wine next to him.

Scythians were nomadic Iranian warriors on horseback from Eurasia, while the semi-nude figure was Dionysus, also known as Bacchus, the Greek god of wine and fertility.

However, even as the ASI revelled in their stupendous finds, along came some shocking news – the government of independent India had decided to build a dam in the valley across the river Krishna.

Why, might you ask?

In 1947, the British left India.

A newly formed Indian union was in the process of creating new infrastructure for its people.

The states of Hyderabad and Madras needed water desperately.

So, a dam and a reservoir were the need of the hour.

Nothing the archaeologists said to dissuade them made a difference.

So, the ASI again swung into action.

Before the Nagarjuna Sagar irrigation project could take off, Operation Salvage was launched.

For six years – from 1954 to 1960 – the ASI dug, and they dug.

They tirelessly excavated to salvage and save whatever they could.

And what a treasure trove it turned out to be!

Among the Maha Chaityas (or prayer halls) unearthed was one with Ikshvaku inscriptions dating back to the second century and earlier, and in that Maha Chaitya, in a small silver stupa within a pearl, garnet and crystal-

Buddha's Relics limestone carving from 3rd–4th century

studded container in a gold casket amidst gold flowers, was a sliver of bone.

Whose bone do you think it was?

You'll be astounded to know it was the Buddha's.

They also found his tooth and a strand of hair.

These were removed quickly to the highest point of the dam, which was the Nagarjunakonda hill that had become an island in the middle of the reservoir.

Remnants of almost thirty odd monasteries were also salvaged before the entire site went underwater.

Nine to fourteen large replicas of the excavated ruins are now on the island. This includes a fourteenth-century fort, some medieval temples and a museum built like a Buddhist Vihara, where a huge Buddha greets you.

The Nagarjuna Sagar Dam was the largest and highest masonry dam in the world at the time.

Sadly, it came at the cost of almost a 100 sites of our ancient heritage that included astonishing relics of the Stone and Medieval Ages.

It was a flourishing ancient kingdom, the ruins of which, though salvaged, have no doubt been lost to us in their original form forever – in the name of modern progress.

The Ikshvaku dynasty appears to have come to a sudden end around 310 CE.

Archaeologists have come up with two plausible reasons.

One – a Pallava invasion. The Pallavas, who ruled most of south India at one time, may have invaded Vijayapuri then pillaged and plundered the capital, ruthlessly smashing all its many beautiful statues and edifices, as almost all of them appear to have been deliberately destroyed.

Two – a raging Krishna River. The river may have angrily overrun its banks during heavy rains, flooding and destroying the city and its environs because the destruction seems to be in keeping with such an occurrence as well.

Whatever the reason, Vijayapuri declined quickly after that.

We know that, as its power waned, the Ikshvakus were eventually followed by the Gajapati Rajus of Odisha, and then the Devaraya rulers of the Vijayanagar Empire, before becoming a part of the Qutub Shahi kingdom and the Mughal Empire.

After that, the once-prominent seat of Buddhism went into a permanent decline, to be finally submerged in independent India and lost to us for eternity.

With many of its excavated sculptures having found their way to the museums of Delhi, Chennai, Kolkata, Paris and New York, and with other artefacts preserved on top of a hill on an island, ancient Nagarjunakonda now rests submerged under the waters of the Nagarjuna Sagar Reservoir of Andhra Pradesh in the Krishna River basin.

How sad is that!

Where is it located: Guntur District of Andhra Pradesh

Timeframe of Settlement: Third century CE–1955

Who discovered it and when:

Suraparaju Venkataramayya, a schoolteacher, in 1926; ASI between 1926–1955

18

SHANGRI-LA

When fiction replaces truth...

The Royal Air Force plane lurched sickeningly.

In a tailspin, it hurtled down at an alarming speed.

Bounced right out of their seats, the four frightened passengers, clung on for dear life clutching the straps and the sides of the aircraft.

As the aircraft crashed to the ground, its wing broke off on impact and its tyres skidded before exploding.

Then all went dark and quiet.

The passengers slowly picked themselves off the plane's floor, checked themselves to see if their limbs were all intact and then gingerly felt their way to the cockpit.

The pilot, still buckled to his seat, was unconscious and bleeding.

They carried him out through the door that had broken off in the crash and laid him on the ground outside.

It was bitterly cold and there was not another soul in sight.

How could there be?

On their way from Baskul in China to Peshawar in Pakistan under British rule, they were stranded high up – no one knew exactly where – among the grey peaks of an isolated range of mountains.

Just then, the pilot opened his eyes.

In answer to their anxious queries, struggling to breath, he haltingly mumbled, 'In Tibet... the Kunlun Mountains. Further down is a valley called Shangri-La. There's a lamasery. Make your way there. You'll be safe.'

Then, drawing a long, shuddering breath, he closed his eyes and died.

Shocked but determined to save themselves, onward to Shangri-La the air-crash victims trudged.

When they arrived at Shangri-La, they discovered that it was a monastery – a haven of peace and calm – where Buddhist gurus or teachers, called lamas, lived.

There was no discord or disharmony or conflict or crime amongst them.

It was the valley of the Blue Moon, where no one grew old or fell ill, where no suffering existed.

Whoever lived there remained the age they were when they entered the monastery.

The head priest was a 250-year-old Frenchman – perhaps even older.

The only catch: if you left the confines of the valley, you would revert to your true age, grow old and die.

It was a paradise – a place unknown to the rest of the world.

So, what do you think? Could there actually be a place like Shangri-La – a place filled with peace and harmony, where nobody aged or died?

If only there were.

No. Shangri-La was an imaginary, fictitious place created by author James Hilton in his 1933 book, *Lost Horizon*.

As was the air crash and its stranded passengers.

Although it was just a figment of Hilton's imagination, Shangri-La captured the imagination of the world – especially after it was made into a hit movie.

Explorers – including the Nazis – began to flock to Tibet in search of this place of perpetual youth, peace and harmony.

They flew, hiked and trekked to find this lost paradise on earth.

No one was prepared to believe it was fictitious or imaginary.

Hotels named after Shangri-La sprang up.

So did holiday resorts, rest houses, music bands, documentaries on lost paradises and buildings.

China even renamed one of its towns Shangri-La to cash in on its popularity and attract tourists.

Amazing, isn't it, the way the world reacts – even to fiction?

Now, in the Himalayas, in one of the remotest parts of Tibet – cut off from the world and on a high plateau encircled by a string of some eight or so mountains – lies a place supposedly called Shambhala.

The Tibetans believe it to be sacred.

They believe it to be a place of peace, harmony, knowledge and rejuvenation – free from all evil.

Free from all suffering too, it allegedly lies in the shadow of a white crystal mountain, beside a lake and a palace.

In Sanskrit, the name Shambhala means 'origin of happiness'.

So, it's a placc where no arrogance, anger, hatred, jealousy or greed exists.

Everybody lives in harmony, filled with love and compassion.

It is home to highly evolved and enlightened monks who have achieved spiritual perfection. They live, study and meditate in Shambhala's isolation and tranquillity.

And when the world faces complete mayhem and destruction, they will, it is believed come out to save humanity.

The truth, however, is that nobody today really knows where Shambhala is.

No, not even the Tibetans themselves.

Buddhists and Hindus however do believe a place like that exists somewhere.

So, James Hilton may well have been inspired by this legendary Tibetan lost valley of peaceful harmony, and decided to make his novel about a similar but imaginary one – Shangri-La.

So, a mythical Shambhala may exist, but Hilton's Shangri-La most definitely does not.

Today, however, they've become synonymous, and one has come to mean the other.

Many have braved the harsh terrain and treacherous weather in the daunting mountains of Tibet, Nepal, Bhutan and even Mongolia in their quest for this tranquil paradise on earth.

Although none have found even an iota of evidence of any such hidden kingdom anywhere, the world continues to be tantalized and fascinated by the very idea of its existence.

And the search for Shambhala – or Shangri-La, the lost valley of perpetual youth and harmony – continues.

Wouldn't you like to find it too?

Where is it located: Kunlun Mountains, Tibet
Timeframe of Settlement: Unknown
Who discovered it and when: Undiscovered

19

TAKSHASHILA

When lost in antiquity...

Thirty-five kilometres from Islamabad (Pakistan) is a lost city.

It is an ancient city with an intriguingly ancient lineage.

It was called Takshashila, and you will never guess who founded it!

If you know the story of Rama, you will remember Bharat, his younger brother.

The same Bharat who ruled Ayodhya on Rama's behalf for fourteen long years, until Rama returned with his wife Sita after killing Ravana, who had kidnapped her.

Yes, this Bharat founded the city, named it after his son Taksha, and made him king there, says the Ramayana.

He also founded Pushkalavati nearby and installed his other son, Pushkala, as ruler.

Takshashila and Pushkalavati (known today as Chārsadda) were – at different times – both capitals of the ancient Gandhara kingdom that now lies in present-day Pakistan and Afghanistan.

Gandhara was also the homeland of Gandhari, the wife and queen of King Dhritarashtra and mother of the Kauravas of the other great Indian epic, the Mahabharata.

It was also where the story of the Mahabharata was narrated for the very first time.

King Janamejaya, the great-grandson of the Pandava prince Arjuna, reportedly held a *sarpa yagna* (grand snake sacrifice) in Takshashila.

At that *yagna*, the sage Vaisampayana related the happenings of the great war – the Mahabharata – to King Janamejaya.

Dictated to Ganesha by the revered Guru Vyasa, the Mahabharata is the tale of the war between two sets of royal cousins – the Kauravas and the Pandavas – over their right to the kingdom of Hastinapur.

At 1,00,000 verses, it is the longest epic poem ever written.

Astounding, isn't it, that all of this should unfold in what is now Pakistan and not India?

Well back then it was all one vast family of kingdoms.

Just as today's Nepal was once the kingdom of Sita's father, Janaka, in ancient times, so too was present-day Pakistan part of a greater India.

Takshashila, meaning 'rock of Taksha' or 'hewn from rock', was thus an important part of that ancient Indian landscape.

Strategically placed along a busy global trade route, Takshashila was also a highly respected centre of learning, says Fa-Hein, a Chinese traveller from the fifth century CE. He was among many who visited this wealthy and flourishing city, famous for its renowned university.

Older than Nalanda in Bihar, Takshashila was not a residential university, nevertheless, it attracted students and visiting faculty from across Asia, Arabia, China and even Greece.

As many as 10,000 day scholars could pursue up to sixteen years of intense study, combining religious lessons with the arts, architecture, sciences, mathematics, philosophy, astronomy, medicine, politics and military warfare.

Intriguingly, the curriculum also included archery, hunting and elephant lore too.

Panini, the great Sanskrit grammarian; Chanakya, the famed political strategist; Patanjali, the yoga guru; and Charaka, the pioneer of Ayurvedic medicine, have all supposedly studied or taught there.

Now, Takshashila, after the epic age, has had a rather chequered and interesting history.

It was first a part of Persia's Achaemenid Empire; then it was conquered by the Greeks under Alexander the Great.

After that, it became a part of the Mauryan Empire, and under Emperor Ashoka, reached its peak as a great centre of Buddhist learning.

It then fell into the hands of the Indo-Greeks (or Bactrian Greeks), the Scythians, then the Parthians, the Kushans and finally, during the Gupta period, the Huns, who brutally destroyed it in the fifth century CE.

It did, however, limp on briefly under the Hindu Shahi rule until the tenth century CE, or so.

Nevertheless, with the Huns began Takshashila's true decline into history.

The Hephthalites, otherwise known as the Huns, were savage nomadic tribes who lived near China.

They were keen on expanding their domain.

So, one group went westward towards Rome and the other to India.

Called the White Huns and known for their barbaric cruelty, they repeatedly attacked India until they finally broke through, and Takshashila came under the control of the Huns' ruler, Mihirakula.

Mihirakula then took great pleasure in systematically destroying all Buddhist and Hindu learning centres.

He also savagely burned and demolished temples and more than 1,500 monasteries and stupas.

Soon Takshashila – referred to as Taxila by the Greeks – was no longer the 1,000-year-old global intellectual power it once was.

Having lost its importance and been reduced to ruins, Takshashila lapsed into obscurity.

It lay forgotten and buried in its own dust for the next few centuries.

Then, in the nineteenth century, having read the accounts of Fa-Hein and other travellers, such as the Greek Megasthenes and Chinese Xuanzang, and their descriptions of the city, the father of Indian archaeology, Sir Alexander Cunningham, went looking for it.

He travelled through India along the ancient pilgrim routes of Chinese monks and others in search of this great centre of learning he had read and heard of so often.

To his delight, he found some ancient ruins on the banks of a tributary of the River Indus – Tamara Nala – in a place called Saraikala near today's Taxila.

He began to excavate the site.

Ten long years of excavation told him that all the write-ups about the once-scholarly city were true.

He began uncovering remnants of different periods in the various layers of soil, one after the other.

Artefacts specific to each culture and kingdom were revealed.

If Corinthian pillars or Alexander's statue popped out, he knew it had to be the Greek period of rule.

If a statue of Buddha or Emperor Ashoka was found, it told him it was from Mauryan times.

Thus, he and his team were able to work out the time of each ruler or kingdom's reign.

After him, the next head of the ASI, John Marshall, carried on the good work.

Four main settlements or cities and three main stupas were found among the remnants of the Taxila ruins.

- The prehistoric mound of Saraikala is the earliest settlement of Takshashila.
- Remnants of pottery shards, tools and so on indicate Neolithic, Stone, Bronze and Iron Ages.
- Bhir Mound – sixth century BCE, the next oldest, with its irregular pattern of houses and streets, had a pillared hall where the Mahabharata may have been first recited, and perhaps where Alexander made his triumphant entry into Taxila in 326 BCE.
- Sirkap – the well-planned, second-century BCE capital on the opposite bank of the river from Taxila – belonged to the Indo-Greek period.
- Sirsukh – the fourth-century CE city from the Kushan period was more modern in comparison to the others.

"*The Dharmarajika Stupa*"

As for the stupas they were simply amazing.

- Dharmarajika Stupa, circular with a raised platform around its base, had a ring of small chapels surrounding it, one of which had an inscribed silver scroll and a gold casket with a relic of Buddha from the Kushan period.
- Kunala Stupa, named after the blind wandering saint and son of Emperor Ashoka, was, yes, Mauryan.
- Jaulian Stupa in Sirsukh, not Buddhist, but with some monasteries around its mound as well as massive sandstone Ionic-Greek style columns, pilasters and Buddha statues, was probably Scytho-Parthian.

Takshashila, once part of undivided India, is today a UNESCO World Heritage Site – all eighteen sites unearthed so far.

The Takshashila ruins are amazing, but sadly, they remind us of the greatness of an intellectual past that's lost to us.

Where is it located: Punjab, Pakistan.
Timeframe of Settlement: Fifth century BCE – Sixth century CE
Who discovered it and when: Sir Alexander Cunningham between 1863–64

What is a Civilization?

- Other than your bond of friendship, what is it that you have in common with your friend who sits beside you in class, or say another friend from another class?
- Your food? They're from another state, say Kerala – and you're from Punjab. So, no.
- Your language? You speak Punjabi and they, Malayalam – no, again.
- Your festivals? No. Not even the clothes you wear to celebrate them are common.
- However, what you do have in common is that the both of you are Indian.
- And you belong to a country called India. You're thus linked together because of a commonality of who you are and the country you belong to.
- And that is what – in the larger context – makes up a civilization.
- So, a civilization is a society with, say, common religious or other cultural beliefs or way of life, hailing from the same geographical area with similar habits, even though at times within it, language and food may differ.

20

INDUS VALLEY CIVILIZATION

When an entire civilization is lost...

Long, long ago, much before the India we know and live in existed, there flourished among the mountains, valleys, rivers and plains of Pakistan, northwestern India, and northeast Afghanistan, an ancient urban civilization.

For about 5,000 years, this civilization thrived and flourished, supposedly in three phases – early pastoral period, the mature or the urban/city phase and the later phase during which it declined and slowly disappeared around the year 1300 BCE.

Its cities then vanished off the face of the earth, to become buried under humungous mounds of mud and debris across the land.

They lay abandoned, lost and forgotten for 3,500 years and more.

Then suddenly, in the nineteenth century, in British India, they were, one by one, accidentally stumbled upon and discovered.

Although ancient, they were so advanced and urban, it astonished archaeologists.

They had well-designed and well-fortified cities, food-storage granaries and a very effective irrigation and water system.

Archaeologists dug out beautifully laid-out streets, double-storeyed houses and buildings that displayed a neat efficiency we would do well to copy.

While houses were of different sizes, with state-of-the-art bath, toilet and sewage systems that indicated a heightened sense of hygiene, the baked bricks used to build them were amazingly of a standard size, similar to ours.

If you assumed they weren't farmers or even into manufacturing, you would be surprised. The land was fertile too.

Discovered among the agricultural produce were remnants of wheat, barley, peas and dates along with pottery kilns, copper furnaces, tools, jewellery, beads and other finished products.

Then there were all those numerous seals and artefacts – both foreign and local – that popped up.

They pointed to internal trade links within the subcontinent as well as outside.

Gold, ivory, timber, cotton textiles, copper and bronze items, weights, precious-stone beads, food grains and even chicken and water buffaloes were exported abroad in return for silver, tin and copper ingots, minerals, woollen textiles and bitumen.

And how do we know that?

Just as Iranian, Mesopotamian, Persian, Omani and Bahraini artefacts were found here, astonishingly, ancient artefacts like stone weights and lapis lazuli beads from here were also found in archaeological digs in those countries as well.

Their mode of transport – bullock carts, watercraft planks with sails and boats, both large and small.

Guess what their toys were like?

Whistles in the shape of birds, small animals with movable heads, toy carts and mazes in clay, just like the plastic and wooden ones you may have played with as five-year-olds.

They also appeared to have been peaceful landowners, carpenters, masons, merchants, coppersmiths, boat builders and even priests, although there was no evidence of a common religion or of any divine kings or emperors.

The first two finds were the cities of Harappa and Mohenjo-daro in the Indus/Ghaggar-Hakra Valley river basin.

So, John Marshall, the then chief of the Archaeological Survey of British India, decided to name it the 'Indus Valley Civilization'.

And in the September 20th, 1924, issue of the *Illustrated London News* announced to the world the discovery of a new ancient hitherto-unknown civilization – as ancient as Mesopotamia (3500 BCE), or Egypt (3100 BCE).

It caused a sensation.

The world wanted to know more about this lost civilization.

Why had it disappeared?

Why had its cities been abandoned and forgotten?

Why were they being found under mound-like hillocks?

Marshall didn't know, nor did anyone else.

Even to this day, it remains an enigma or mystery our experts have long been trying to unravel.

To date, over a thousand similar sites have been unearthed across India, which tell us that the civilization was more widespread than we ever imagined.

In 2016, scientists from ASI and the Indian Institute of Technology (IIT) found evidence in Bhirrana, Haryana, and elsewhere that pointed to the lost civilization being even older than previously believed.

Also discovered in the Gulf of Khambhat/Cambay, off the Arabian Sea coast of Gujarat, India, were human remains – fossils and artefacts of Indus/Harappan origin – that could well go back 9,000-odd years, that is, predating the Mahabharata age.

Another whopping surprise to the world, wouldn't you say?

The actual origin of the Indus Valley Civilization, it is believed, may be in Mehrgarh, in the foothills of modern-day Balochistan in western Pakistan.

There appears to have been a settlement there as early as 7000 BCE, long before Harappa and Mohenjo-daro.

Thus, not only could the Indus Valley/Harappan Civilization – found first in Harappa – be geographically the largest, over 1 million sq. km, but also by far the oldest.

Now, recent excavations in Rakhigarhi, Haryana, hint at even more stunning revelations.

So, let us swing by a few Harappan cities, shall we, and find out what they're all about before we meet up with the Harappans at Rakhigarhi?

Where is it located: Pakistan, northwestern India, northeast Afghanistan and Iran

Timeframe of Settlement: 3300 BCE–1300 BCE

21

HARAPPA

When rivers change course...

Harappa. The first clue that led to the mysterious Indus Valley/Harappan Civilization.

Harappa. The archaeological discovery that changed the history of India.

Harappa. The city that lay in our own backyard, now in Pakistan.

And it was first introduced to the world by the chief of the Archaeological Survey of British India, John Marshall, exactly 100 years ago.

However, it was a soldier, a collector of coins (a numismatist), who chanced upon it long before Marshall did.

He was James Lewis of the British East India Company army, who was posted in Agra in the early nineteenth century.

A keen collector of old artefacts and ancient coins, he was a bit of a rebel.

So, one day, he decided to desert or run away from the army.

He changed his name to Charles Masson, and, for the next ten years and more, was on the run.

Picking up artefacts and coins from ancient ruins and caves, he travelled through Punjab, Sindh, Rajasthan, Baluchistan, Iran and Afghanistan.

And, in 1829, when he landed up at a place called Harappa by the River Ravi in the Punjab, he came upon some humungous but intriguing old mounds.

He wondered what they held.

Could it be more precious coins or even some jewels?

Digging around, to his great disappointment, he found no coins but some brick ruins.

Even so, he made some detailed drawings of the area.

'Could these ruins be from the time of Alexander the Great's India campaign in 326 BCE?' he wondered.

They were not.

They were even more ancient, but he wasn't to know that.

Anyway, delighted with some 80,000 coins he had already collected earlier, and surprisingly having gotten the army to pardon him for having deserted, he decided to head home.

Back in England, Masson published his findings.

It caught the eye of Alexander Cunningham, the first chief of ASI, India, and he decided to check it out.

And how did he do that?

On bullock carts, horses, elephants, camels and even on foot, he traversed the expanse, making copious notes and mapping the ruins.

He looked for coins, inscriptions, sculptures and interviewed the locals.

He then excavated Masson's mysterious Harappan mounds.

And guess what?

He found the first engraved animal image – on Harappan soapstone seals.

He was mystified.

'What were these seals for?' he wondered.

He soon realized that they were used to stamp and seal letters and bags.

Amazingly, there were different seals for different purposes and different senders.

They came in all shapes – round, square, rectangular.

What did these famous seals actually look like?

Wrote Sir Alexander Cunningham, in 1872:

> *The most curious object discovered at Harappa is a seal... The seal is a smooth black stone without polish... On it is engraved very deeply a bull, without a hump, looking to the right, with two stars under the neck...*
>
> *Note on Harappa* by Sir Alexander Cunningham, pp. 105–108

However, at the time, Cunningham didn't know how ancient it was – nor whom it had belonged to.

The village of Harappa, according to local lore, had once been part of the legendary kingdom of a wicked Raja Har Pal, who was reportedly killed in a storm that destroyed the city.

Hence the name 'Harappa'.

Cunningham too recorded his findings.

Then, when John Marshall became head of the ASI, he decided to take a closer look at what had been discovered at Harappa.

So, in 1921–1922, off went Daya Ram Sahni from the ASI to conduct a full-scale excavation – and what he uncovered took Marshall by surprise.

The huge, parallelogram-shaped mound, once excavated, revealed a full-fledged, well-fortified settlement; an ancient but remarkably advanced and well-laid urban city – complete with towers and gateways enclosed by a mudbrick wall.

Spread over 370 acres along the River Ravi in the Indus River basin, it was a raised citadel complex and a lower town consisting of official and residential units with elaborate drainage, sanitation and water systems – that included wells, tanks and terracotta drainpipes.

'How could they have had the means to build something so advanced so long ago?' he wondered.

There were flat-roofed, fired brick houses of red sand and clay, massive granaries for storage and, yes, cemeteries – but no temples, palaces or armouries were found.

Then, much to his disbelief, he discovered artefacts like perfume bottles and jewellery remarkably similar to those found in ancient Iran, Mesopotamia, Egypt and Syria.

So, whoever had lived here, Marshall realized, must have lived well and had strong international trade links.

So evidently, they loved to doll up and smell great and were good craftsmen too.

Also found were numerous female figurines, pottery, copper tools and clay or stone tablets with writing.

However, unlike hieroglyphics or cuneiform, the writing couldn't be deciphered.

“Hand-modelled terracotta figurines from Harappa”

And the trident-shaped, plant-like markings – that appear to be written from right to left – continue to perplex our experts.

When carbon dated – a method by which the age of an object can be determined – the artefacts and ruins were found to belong to the Bronze Age (3300–3200 BCE), as old as Mesopotamia or Egypt.

As the excavations continued, Marshall couldn't contain his excitement.

Soon after, however, the Partition of India in 1947 happened.

British India was divided into two independent countries – India and Pakistan.

Harappa went with Pakistan, but excavations continued across the rest of India, throwing up even more proof of the civilization's existence and antiquity.

Why was ancient Harappa abandoned and forgotten?

Why was it found under those mounds?

Nobody really knows.

There were no signs of any invasion or war, or of any outsiders having taken over.

Nor were there any weapons of destruction found, or signs of a sudden collapse.

So then, could it have been climate change – famine, flooding, or the River Ravi changing course – that might have caused the Harappans to move in search of more fertile land to farm and feed themselves?

Quite possibly, say experts.

Drastic climate change may have forced them to gradually move away.

However, the town of Harappa, rebuilt over parts of its ancient ruins, still exists today.

It was a site that was inadvertently damaged quite badly by the British, who used many of the ancient, uniformly sized bricks found among the ruins to build India's first railway line.

As more and more Harappan cities come to light, they just might one day reveal the full story of what truly happened to Harappa as well.

Until then, the disappearance of ancient Harappa will probably continue to intrigue and baffle our experts.

Where is it located: Sahiwal district, Punjab, Pakistan

Timeframe of Settlement: 3300 BCE–1500 BCE

Who discovered it and when:

Charles Masson in 1829;

Alexander Cunningham in 1872;

ASI in 1921

Some misconceptions about archaeology:

1. You have to dig deep to find ancient artefacts.

No, it depends on the land site. They have often been found just below the surface as well.

2. Archaeologists get to keep the treasures found.

No. They need to hand them in to the authorities.

3. Archaeologists study dinosaurs.

No, archaeologists might discover dinosaurs, but they study remains of past people. Palaeontologists and geologists study dinosaurs.

4. Archaeology is easy.

No, it is a scientific field that needs specialized study.

22

MOHENJO-DARO

When river levels rise, or disease spreads...

Rakhal Das Banerji was with the Archaeological Survey of British India.

He was an intrepid explorer who loved his work.

Checking out monuments and ruins – he was constantly on the move.

On one such trip, he happened to spot some mysterious mounds in a distance.

They were along the River Indus, in the Larkana district of Sindh.

At first, he thought they might be old Buddhist stupas.

Intrigued, he was determined to check them out.

So, to Dokri – its nearest railway station – he went.

The mounds were still some 15 km away.

He jumped into a *tonga* – a horse-drawn two-wheeled carriage – that took him only part of the way.

Unfazed, he covered the rest of the distance on foot.

To his amazement, he came across not just a few, but many rolling mounds.

And at the centre of it all stood two large citadels – silent, imposing and full of mystery.

Now, a year earlier, along the River Ravi in the valley of the River Indus, a momentous discovery in Harappa, some 600 km away, had had the ASI enthralled.

Banerji's colleague, Daya Ram Sahni, had discovered an ancient, urbanized city under a large citadel.

Daya Ram had also found more of those unique seals that had been discovered earlier by the then ASI head, Alexander Cunningham, who hadn't known just how ancient they were.

They had since been found to be from 3200 BCE – as old as Mesopotamia or Egypt.

'Could these vast mounds, made of similar burnt bricks, be holding something as old or unique?' he wondered hopefully.

So, he set to work to uncover their secrets.

The mounds were, however, better preserved than Harappa's.

Of the two mounds that stood out, one citadel was smaller but higher, and the other, lower but larger.

The villagers called them *Mohenjo-daro* – the mound of the dead.

Unearthed, they appeared to cover a well-fortified city of some 7 km.

As the excavation proceeded, an astonished Banerji grew more and more excited.

Out tumbled seals similar to the ones found by Alexander Cunningham in Harappa.

'Could it possibly have been the same civilization?' he asked himself in wonder.

It was more than what he had hoped for.

Unable to contain his excitement, he sent word to his boss, John Marshall, Director General of ASI:

> *Three different seals bearing the bull statant with a standard in front have been discovered. They are exactly similar to Cunningham's Harappa seals. Two of these belong to the same period...*

Thrilled anticipation coursed through the ASI.

Were they on the cusp of discovering something huge?

Had they hit upon an ancient civilization hitherto unknown?

It would seem so.

More discoveries followed, and it was proved beyond the shadow of a doubt that the people who had lived in Mohenjo-daro were similar to those who had lived in Harappa.

Everything discovered was similar – similar structures, similar artefacts, similar houses, similar granaries, and yes, it had public baths too, just like Harappa.

In fact, the excavated Great Bath, with stairs descending on two sides into a large, rectangular, brick-lined courtyard, was actually the most distinguishing feature of the Mohenjo-daro excavation.

It even had fitted bricks and waterproof bitumen.

Most homes also had indoor bathrooms with flushing toilets.

It was a state-of-the-art sewage system that could teach us a thing or two.

It was undoubtedly a carefully planned, stylish city where hygiene was important.

Even the script was common, and as for the soapstone seals engraved with unicorns, elephants, rhinos, buffalos, crocodiles, bulls, antelopes and hares, they were Harappan too.

Stunned by these discoveries, John Marshall realized it was a whole new lost civilization.

A mysterious lost civilization of perhaps many cities with similar structures and culture, and not just one lost city of Harappa.

And that was how a happy John Marshall, calling it the 'Indus Valley Civilization', announced to the world that a new civilization as old as any had been discovered in the Indus River valley in India, now popularly referred to as the Harappan civilization.

Among the thousands of artefacts discovered were items of pottery, copper and stone tools, toys, games, jewellery and weights.

Along with gold, terracotta and stone figurines found was a figure of a priest-king in a beard and a designer robe and an 11-cm-tall bronze figurine of a dancing girl striking a pose, sporting attitude and a necklace.

Among the seals, there was one with a Shiva-like figure surrounded by animals.

Again, like at Harappa, there was no evidence of any palace or temple or even a weaponized army.

The Mohenjo-daro settlement, however, was twice the size of Harappa.

Then, to his surprise, Banerji also found a whole lot of skeletons.

No wonder the locals referred to it as *Mohenjo-daro* or 'mound of the dead', he thought.

Skeletons lay scattered on the streets below and within houses.

Several lay in strange, twisted postures, amidst layers of ash and rubble.

Could they have died violent deaths?

It appeared totally different from what seemed to have happened in Harappa.

Had there been an invasion after all?

Did outsiders, like the Aryans, conquer and invade them?

Did marauders swoop in from the north, sweep over the city and then pass on, leaving the dead lying where they fell?

Sir Mortimer Wheeler, who became the ASI chief later on, believed this was so.

He was convinced that that was how Mohenjo-daro had fallen and finally disappeared.

However, there was nothing to show that they had died of conflict or war wounds.

None of the skeletons bore any such injuries.

Nor were any weapons of war found. Not one.

It didn't seem as if they had fought any war, and the lack of evidence was glaring.

There was evidence, however, of a peaceful society engaged in trade and agriculture.

So, the invasion theory has since been discarded.

So, what could have happened to the people of urban Mohenjo-daro?

Flooding is what archaeologists now believe happened.

The clayey, silt-filled alluvial soil indicated that extensive flooding had often taken place.

The whole city seemed to have been deliberately built on a higher level as if to protect itself from rising water levels.

The Indus River was known to change its course and, through the centuries, had gradually moved.

That could easily have been the probable cause.

Could water-borne diseases have spread after the flooding, killing the people?

Maybe one final flood or even several mini floods could have caused many to drown or die of illness and others to leave, surmised experts.

They may have emigrated to set up new homes elsewhere.

Mohenjo-daro, for example, lay to the south of Harappa.

And that is where it rests today.

In 1947, when India was partitioned, Harappa and Mohenjo-daro became part of Pakistan.

Now Pakistan wanted to keep all that was excavated from Harappa and Mohenjo-daro.

India refused.

So, the artefacts – even bits of pottery – were split equally down the middle.

The Priest-King went to Pakistan, and the Dancing Girl came to India along with the Pasupati-Shiva Seal.

So, thanks to Banerji, we now had a whole new ancient but lost civilization to ponder over.

Pop by the National Museum, New Delhi, or the various on-site museums, plus some in the

“ *The Priest-King* ”

“ *The Dancing Girl* ”

"The Pasupati-Shiva Seal"

US, France, the UK and Pakistan, to check out the Indus Valley artefacts Banerji and his colleagues have found. You'll be surprised at their detail.

Where is it located: Pakistan

Timeframe of Settlement: 2600 BCE–1500 BCE

Who discovered it and when:

Rakhal Das Banerji/John Marshall in 1922;

Mortimer Wheeler in 1945;

George F. Dales in 1965

23

DHOLAVIRA

When white sands take over…

Dholavira.

The very name has a musical ring to it, doesn't it?

The sound of beating drums, dancing feet and even twirling skirts perhaps?

A happy medley.

However, lyrical as the word Dholavira may sound, its meaning is somewhat more mundane.

In Gujarati, it translates as 'waterholes in a river with a white sand bed'.

What does that even mean, right?

Well, Dholavira is the last village on the western tip of Khadir Bet (*bet* means island) – in the Great Rann of Kutch, that sits on the Tropic of Cancer.

The locals refer to Dholavira simply as *Kotada Timbo*, meaning 'Fort Mound'.

And that is exactly what it has been for the last 4,000 years and more.

It would have continued to remain so but for the efforts of a local inhabitant, Shambhudan Gadhvi.

Now, what is this Great Rann of Kutch?

Rann means 'desert' in Hindi, and the Great Rann, one of the largest salt marshes in the world, spreads over 7,850 sq. km along Gujarat's borders and the Thar Desert that abuts Pakistan.

The Great Rann, together with Little Rann of Kutch (4,950 sq. km), also in Gujarat, is referred to as the Rann of Kutch.

Although it's surrounded by many tributaries from as far above north as the Indus River emptying into the Arabian Sea, the Rann was once a part of the Arabian Sea that dried up when the sea receded, leaving behind its salt.

This then became a vast, silvery-white expanse of dry, arid land.

Thus, for the inhabitants, if the rains failed and there was no water saved, Kotada in the Great Rann of Kutch would go dry.

So, it was during one such season that Shambhudan Gadhvi, a local small-time geologist, was supervising the digging of a small dam to collect monsoon waters.

As they dug, they came across a strange artefact.

It had on it an animal image that looked familiar.

'Where have I seen this before?,' he asked himself. Ahhh, yes, he had seen it in a book.

So, he rushed home and in his little son's history book found an exact image of what he held in his hand.

It was a Harappan seal – some 3,500 years old.

Excited beyond belief, he went back and dug some more.

Out tumbled scores of similar little items. Soon, his backyard was filled with such artefacts.

He was convinced that there was something much bigger beneath the ground.

It, however, took him many years to convince the authorities to look into it.

Finally, the ASI sent in their excavators and soon the dig was swarming with excited archaeologists.

What gradually popped out was a spectacularly well-preserved, well-planned, urban city on a hundred hectares of semi-arid land.

Located at the tri-junction of water routes from Sindh, Rajasthan and Kutch, it was a walled settlement with a fortified castle, a ceremonial ground, a cemetery, a citadel, a middle town and a lower town, nine uniquely designed gates and, yes, a stadium with terraced stands – all Harappan in style.

It had a series of cascading freshwater reservoirs – some sixteen of them – lined with stone, in the east and south of the Fort Mound citadel.

And those reservoirs were probably what the 'water holes in a river with a white sand bed' meant and what Dholavira was all about.

There was no potable groundwater, so two now-extinct rivulets – the Mansar and the Manhar – were probably diverted and dammed, and their waters, along with fresh rainwater, collected in these reservoirs.

Pits and wells, drains and canals to store and channel water, along with well-laid underground sewage pipes also surfaced.

Their main occupation appeared to have been agriculture and cattle rearing.

As the groundwater was salty, much of the agriculture had to rely on rainwater – which explains the need for such an elaborate water-storage system.

The Dholavira water-management system was one of the most efficient and sophisticated setups yet seen among the lost cities.

And guess what?

A massive stepwell – three times the size of the Great Bath of Mohenjo-daro – was also unearthed here.

Yes, along with what could well be the world's earliest signboard – with ten large stone inscriptions carved in the Indus Valley script.

Unfortunately, nobody has been able to decipher it yet.

While everything else was similar to Harappa, there was one major difference: instead of baked and burnt bricks, the buildings here were made of sandstone.

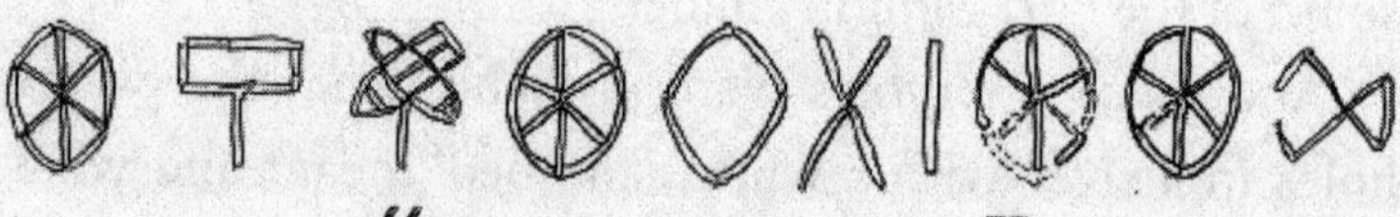

"The Dholavira Signboard"

Workshops and copper smelters, also found here, suggest they were into manufacturing and trading internationally – as tools from Oman, the UAE and Mesopotamia were discovered at the site.

As usual, the question on every archaeologist's mind was:

Why had such a thriving settlement declined?

Why had it been lost?

And just as frequently, the answer that came up was – drastic climatic change.

With rivers in the Indus Valley shifting and drying up – like the Saraswati River – and as flow from its tributaries, among them the Rupen and Luni, reduced, Dholavira must have faced severe drought conditions.

So, people in Harappa may have started moving out.

That might have been the time when the other great civilization, Mesopotamia, was also declining, and trade between the two could have dried up.

It must have forced the people of Dholavira, too, to seek out other avenues to survive.

The Arabian Sea, which once came right up to the Great Rann of Kutch, likely receded around that time, drying out the land, making it barren or inundated with salt.

It forced them to perhaps give up their two main occupations – agriculture and maritime trade.

Unable to provide food, raw materials and products for markets at home and abroad, their economy probably declined sharply.

Thus, Dholavira – the fifth largest and the most spectacular of the Harappan excavation sites so far in India – was also, perhaps, simply abandoned.

There was no dramatic collapse or invasion.

The lack of freshwater – due to monsoon failure, rivers changing course or drying up and the onset of a severe drought – perhaps finally got the better of them.

So, like the other Harappan cities, the inhabitants must've simply upped and left.

They may have moved further south into Gujarat, or perhaps even into Maharashtra and beyond.

With a UNESCO World Heritage Site tag, Kotada even today has no proper drinking water.

The salty desert plains of the Great Rann, however, seem to be home to the chinkara, gazelle, nilgai and flamingos.

Where is it located: Khadir Bet in Bhachau Taluka of Kutch, Gujarat

Timeframe of Settlement: 2650 BCE–1450 BCE

Who discovered it and when: ASI in 1967

24

KALIBANGAN

When rivers dry up...

Say you've been living in a place comfortably for years and years.

It's on the banks of a river that provides you with more than enough water for all your needs.

With plentiful crops for food and trade, and healthy cattle for milk and warmth, you have no worries in the world.

Then suddenly there's an earthquake – maybe some horrific landslides and massive floods.

And just like that, your home is lost.

The river that was once your lifeline is now a trickle, choked by stones, rocks and pebbles.

Your grazing pastures are no longer green and flourishing.

They're filled with rubble and debris.

Now you have no shelter, no proper water and no food.

What do you do?

You go in search of another home.

So do your neighbours.

All of you now move to a safer place to start life all over again.

And that is perhaps what happened to the people of Kalibangan on the banks of the Ghaggar River in Rajasthan.

Perhaps not quite so dramatically but gradually over the years, as earthquakes happened and monsoons played truant and the river and fields dried up, the inhabitants probably had no choice.

So, abandon Kalibangan they had to.

And there, under mounds of rubble and debris, it lay abandoned and forgotten for several centuries – until, of all people, an Italian first stumbled upon it.

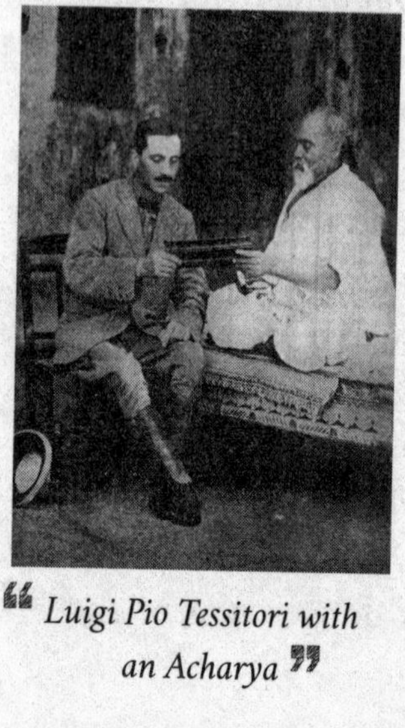

“Luigi Pio Tessitori with an Acharya”

Who was that Italian?

He was Luigi Pio Tessitori, an Indologist and linguist.

Proficient in Pali, Prakrit and Sanskrit, he was keen on studying ancient Indian texts.

Since it was in poetic form, he was interested in establishing Tulsidas's *Ramcharitmanas* as a brand-new work – even though it was based on Valmiki's Ramayana.

He was also interested in old Rajasthani grammar and dialects.

And so, to work in a school in Rajasthan he came.

Poetry or songs by local bards (poets-cum-singers) were a popular form of entertainment in Rajasthan.

So, he joined the Linguistic Survey of India (LSI) and along with other literary outputs produced a bardic and historical survey of Rajputana.

A keen amateur archaeologist, he was soon also scoping out monuments and inscriptions for the ASI.

So, to Jodhpur and Bikaner he went in search of memorial pillars, sculptures and coins and, to his delight, found two huge marble images of the goddess Saraswati near Ganganagar.

Then, in 1918, he discovered a few ancient seals among some mounds in Kalibangan.

That being the time when Harappa was being discovered, he was excited.

They looked remarkably similar to the ones that had been found in Harappa.

So, he immediately wrote to an archaeologist friend about the find.

'Inform John Marshall of the ASI,' his friend wrote back, 'and send him the seals at once.'

However, before he could, Tessitori died of the Spanish flu and was buried in Bikaner.

And Kalibangan remained forgotten once again.

It was some years before his correspondence and papers came to light and the world came to know of what he might have discovered.

The ASI then, some thirty years later, began actual excavations in Kalibangan and the region of the now defunct Ghaggar, otherwise known as the Saraswati River.

The two excavated mounds soon threw up proof that this too had been a Harappan site – particularly similar to Mohenjo-daro in Pakistan.

How could they be sure?

They discovered pottery that matched pottery found there as well as in other Harappan sites.

Pottery that matched in six ways:

(i) in a combination of two colours, i.e. red and black
(ii) incised, i.e. had deep impressions and minute details
(iii) baked, i.e. made using fire.
(iv) rusticated, i.e. with a rough surface
(v) buff, i.e. sometimes containing lime
(vi) greyware, i.e. sometimes grey in colour.

Now, along with brick walls and buildings, if such artefacts – i.e. pottery from excavated sites – matched all six descriptions, then it was deemed Harappan.

So, Kalibangan was declared a Harappan site.

Furthermore, the well-planned, urban, chessboard layout of the city, its double citadels, baths, buildings, drains and fortified walls all pointed to the Harappans having set up home here and then abandoning it.

Again, how and why?

Possibly because the River Ghaggar, also known as the Ghaggar-Hakra, dried up after a few earthquakes.

Remains of sun-baked brick houses, red-black pottery, terracotta artefacts (including a bronze humped bull), alabaster, shells, and ovens like our present-day *tandoors* have been recovered from the riverbed.

The human-like figurines, however, were more realistic than those found in other Harappan sites.

Unearthed were some new structures too – fire altars.

There were rows and rows of fire altars – within buildings – at different levels.

It was a new add-on that quite baffled the experts.

'Could it have played a religious role?' they wondered.

The Kalibangans may have begun worshipping fire, perhaps.

Kalibangan, too, like the rest of the Harappan civilization, must've gone through three phases of survival.

The first phase of pastoral and early village farming saw them lay the foundation of the civilization, as the first known ploughed-up agricultural field was found in Kalibangan.

The second phase was when they became more mature and urban.

The third was probably where it all began to decline and fall apart.

Since no evidence of a war or massacre has so far emerged, drastic climate change must have caused the mass exodus of the people of Kalibangan.

Proof of a massive earthquake during a pre-Harappan age has been found.

So, that must be what happened to our Kalibangan Harappans later as well.

Thus, with repeated earthquakes, and the Ghaggar-Hakra River drying up, changing course or completely disappearing, it may have forced the Kalibangan Harappans to abandon Kalibangan.

With no drinking water and cattle to rear, what option would they have had?

Today, the Ghaggar-Hakra River is a seasonal river – in flow only during the monsoons.

Thus, like all other cities of the Indus Valley Civilization, Kalibangan too was soon lost to us.

Why was it called Kalibangan?

Interestingly, it was named after the heaps of black-coloured (*kali*) terracotta bangle fragments found on the surface of its mounds.

They are usually worn to ward off evil.

Although the disappearance of Kalibangan was also attributed to earthquakes and rivers drying up, it still continues to puzzle.

Where is it located: Hanumangarh district, Rajasthan, 310 km from Delhi

Timeframe of Settlement: 2500 BCE–1750 BCE

Who discovered it and when:
Luigi Pio Tessitori in 1918;
ASI from 1950s onwards

25

LOTHAL

When oceans overrun...

Lothal.

Nope, it isn't a planet in the Outer Rim Territories of any Galactic Empire, nor is it from Star Wars.

It is, however, an ancient port town in the Indian state of Gujarat.

Well, even though it may not be part of an alien galaxy, it's probably the world's first port town on planet Earth.

Oh, okay, if not the very first, it's certainly among the oldest anyway.

And isn't that kind of exciting too?

It was a once-upon-a-time lively, bustling seaside trading town where all kinds of cultures mingled.

Ships from across the world sailed into Lothal's harbour to unload people and goods and then set off again with more people and Indian ware, some 4,000 years ago.

Isn't it mind-boggling to think that what we take for granted so much today was happening so many thousands of years ago as well?

Importantly, it is also the very first Harappan town excavated in independent India.

Harappa, as you know, went with Pakistan when the Partition of India happened.

So, you see, the discovery of Lothal as part of the mysterious and lost Indus Valley/Harappan Civilization is probably as thrilling as finding any place in an alien galactic empire.

Now, in your mind's eye, picture this.

Picture or imagine the five rivers – Ravi, Sutlej, Beas, Chenab and Jhelum – like an umbrella, starting from the Himalayas down to Harappa, and then flowing as one – Indus – to Mohenjo-daro in Pakistan and into Ladakh in India, and then via a network of interconnecting river-links and tributaries to many other Harappan sites including Kalibangan on the Ghaggar-Hakra River in Rajasthan, Rakhigarhi in Haryana and Dholavira in the Rann of Kutch – to finally reach Lothal on the Sabarmati River, way down in Gujarat, before emptying into the Arabian Sea in the Gulf of Khambhat.

Isn't that an amazing distance to cover?

Maybe 3,000 km – maybe more.

And how do we know this?

Through satellite imagery.

Confirmed also by the discovery of ruins along the way and then of an entire city with a marketplace and, yes, an astonishing operational dockyard at Lothal.

Yes, Lothal, with a large, brick-walled dockyard – some 7,800 sq. m large – with a sluice gate that controlled water levels and opened into a canal that led to the sea.

Built on terraced platforms to keep it safe from flooding, it also had a wharf to anchor ships.

Satellite imagery also tells us that the dry, debris-filled patch that had been unearthed here was once the Sabarmati riverbed that shifted and is now 20 km away from where it was initially.

When archaeologist S.R. Rao of the ASI discovered Lothal, he couldn't have been more excited.

First there were the seals, almost sixty-five of them.

They looked Harappan.

Then came the artefacts and tools made of terracotta, copper, iron and bronze – Harappan.

Then there was the layout – fortified upper town, lower town and mud walls with burnt bricks – again Harappan.

“Seals found in Lothal”

Next were the baths, granaries, buildings, houses, drains, wells and paved floors similar to the ones discovered in Harappa.

Every house had a staircase, a kitchen and several rooms just like the other Harappan cities.

Then, to crown it all, a one-of-a-kind dockyard with a warehouse and inlet channels.

That was something new, never found in any Harappan site before.

It was irrefutably however, proved – after carbon dating – that they had all existed at the same time.

Found also were clay models of sophisticated boats, complete with stone anchors and ladders to cabins.

A unique circular Bahraini seal with a dragon motif amid gambolling gazelles, among other foreign artefacts, was recovered.

Popping up along with gems, carnelian and other ornaments from across the world were bead-making workshops.

If you drop in at the Lothal on-site museum, you will get to see a few hundreds of the artefacts recovered here.

Thus, Lothal was probably an important manufacturing hub as well.

A prominent town, with an artificial dockyard where a lot of cotton and rice appear to have been both cultivated and exported.

Overseas traders, say experts, may have come to Gujarat through the Gulf of Khambhat, then gone to Dholavira through an inland river network connected to the Rann of Kutch and then carried goods back to Mesopotamia, the Middle East and Egypt.

So, all in all, it seems to have been a small but very busy trade centre.

All this conclusively proves that all the Indus Valley/ Harappan Civilization cities had river- and sea-trade links not only within the subcontinent of India but abroad as well.

It was probably the world's first known artificial dry dock connected to a river, the Sabarmati, and for all we know, the Indus Valley/Harappan Civilization itself may be in the running to overtake Mesopotamia as the world's oldest river civilization too.

UNESCO believes Lothal must've been as important as any port town of the ancient world.

They classify it with Carthage in Tunisia, Jaffa in Israel and Ur in Mesopotamia.

Now just like Mohenjo-daro, *Lothal* in Gujarati means 'mound of the dead'.

Nobody knows why.

Also, as with all the other Harappan sites, nobody knows for sure why it was lost or abandoned either.

It has puzzled archaeologists since the discovery of the very first sites at Harappa and Mohenjo-daro and continues to do so.

That it wasn't a dramatic collapse or an invasion, is now certain.

So, just like the other Harappan towns, did the weather play a role?

Was Lothal struck by some natural calamity?

It seems so.

Lothal appears to have been submerged and rebuilt many times.

So, the city may have become overcrowded over time, with houses built on top of houses.

With persistent adverse weather conditions, trade and agriculture, on which their livelihood depended, may have been hit too, eventually trickling down to a stop.

And then, even as it slowly declined, a tsunami of tidal water may have struck Lothal.

It may have gushed through its streets, flattening buildings, taking lives, destroying everything in its path until the bustling port town was no more.

Situated more inland today and buried under mounds of debris, salt and silt, it lay lost, forgotten and abandoned for thousands of years, as parts of it still do even today.

How sad is that?

Where is it located: Saragwala Village, 80 km from Ahmedabad, Gujarat

Timeframe of Settlement: 2400 BCE–1900 BCE

Who discovered it and when: ASI in 1954

26

RAKHIGARHI

When civilizations simply spread...

The year – 1997.

The air is rife with excited anticipation.

Huddled around a few mounds is a group of archaeologists.

Unsure as to what they've just unearthed, they examine the pit carefully.

'Was it?' they wonder.

'Could it be?' they hope.

Then comes the nod from the leader.

'Yesss, it is!'

And a victorious cheer goes up.

Some 150 km northwest of modern-day Delhi in Rakhigarhi, renowned archaeologist Amarendra Nath of the ASI and his men have just discovered another Harappan site.

The ASI had known of the site as early as 1963 but it needed Nath, some thirty odd years later, to come, excavate and confirm what they already suspected.

Now, scroll down to 2000–2016.

More excavations followed.

Cheers ring out again.

It is, indeed, the largest Harappan settlement ever found.

And amazing as it is, it is in India.

Spread over 5.5 sq. km, it's larger than Mohenjo-daro in Pakistan – the largest settlement found up until then.

Eleven mounds have been excavated so far.

Each one throwing up more artefacts of Harappan design as never before.

A gold foundry with ornaments and some 3,000 unpolished semi-precious stones; tools for polishing gemstones and a furnace; gold-and-silver vessels, in addition to clay pots of the Harappan kind; some red earthen tableware – a dish-on-a-stand, a vase and a perforated jar – bits of coloured cloth; and then, above all, the seals.

Happily, the Rakhigarhi seals were no different from the seals found in other Harappan sites.

These seals, as you know, were used to stamp and seal bags and messages.

With scripts – still undeciphered – and animals engraved on them, they were unique to Harappa.

With a combination of symbols and images, it was a pictographic script, short, sweet and mysterious.

Almost 600 symbols have been found on seals, small tablets and ceramic pots.

Ongoing research suggests that it could be an ancient Tamil script.

If that's proved true, then once again it would turn our accepted view of history on its head.

Convinced it is akin to the Tamil language, the chief minister of Tamil Nadu, in 2024, offered a one-million-dollar reward to whoever is able to decipher it.

Interestingly, one of the Rakhigarhi seals was cylindrical, with five Harappan characters on one side and an alligator on the other.

Rakhigarhi was thus no different from the other lost cities of the Indus Valley/Harappan Civilization in the Indian subcontinent.

No different in the well-planned, urban-city layout that they went on to unearth.

No different in its state-of-the-art, separate drainage and sewage systems, or the houses and buildings of burnt brick laid out in true Harappan and Mohenjo-daro style.

And no different are the foreign artefacts recovered there either.

Rakhigarhi, located in the Ghaggar-Hakra River plains up north, sat on an ancient trade route.

It must, therefore, have been a vital trade centre, or else how would these pieces have arrived there?

And, as sprawling a settlement as it was, and surrounded by flourishing, fertile fields, it must have been an important agricultural hub as well, bustling with life and energy.

The mounds were quickly numbered, to make them easier to identify.

The remains of some sun-dried brick houses and burnt brick drains and a few fire altars were marked on the first mound unearthed.

Mound two had a high citadel, a granary, a market complex and a few wells.

Mounds three to six had remains of more of the same with a cemetery thrown in.

Under mound seven, however, was a significantly different discovery: in a half-a-metre-deep sand pit were the skeletal remains of a young couple buried together.

A couple who had probably died at the same time.

Facing each other, they appeared to have been more than mere friends.

The remains were remarkably well-preserved, and the experts believe it was a joint burial.

It was unique, and a one-of-a-kind burial.

More graves were then examined – about seventy of them nearby.

However not one had more than a single skeleton.

So, off for some carbon dating – in 2016 – and DNA testing the skeletons were sent, and what did they find? No diseases or injuries, nor any abnormal cause of death.

Also sent for DNA testing were the remains of a woman found among some artefacts.

So, while how the couple died is still a mystery, *when* they and the woman died was not.

An astonishing 4,600 years ago, was the answer.

Their DNA tests also threw up something equally, if not more, stunning.

It was, they said, similar to the DNA of all modern Indians.

How awesome is that!

Subsequent evidence points to the civilization dating back to 7,000 to 8,000 years ago as well.

“ *Skeleton found at Rakhigarhi* ”

So then, how did the city disappear? Why was it lost or abandoned?

Maybe it didn't disappear. Maybe it wasn't abandoned.

There are people living in Rakhigarhi even to this day.

The village lies 27 km away from the now seasonal and more or less defunct Ghaggar-Hakra River or the lost river Saraswati, as it was known then.

Its people live among and on top of the mounds, probably unaware of their history or what's beneath them.

Since the area is still populated, only a small portion has been excavated so far.

The rest of the ancient Harappan site still lies buried beneath the present-day village.

So, maybe Rakhigarhi as a whole wasn't lost, but is still built over unlike other Harappan sites, that had been abandoned.

As the River Ghaggar-Hakra dried up, the fertile lands around it may have gone arid.

With food and water gone, the population may have dwindled or dispersed.

And then, over the centuries, while parts of the old settlement may have gotten covered by layers of mud and debris, Rakhigarhi could be one of those cities that moved but continued nearby, couldn't it?

In other words, they could probably be people who belonged to the same civilization – the Indus valley/ Harappan Civilization – who spread further east or south, but had also, in Rakhigarhi, remained not too far away from their original site.

Looking at Rakhigarhi today, it makes you wonder: could the lifestyle in our villages today have been introduced to us by the ancient Harappans?

As we apply newer techniques to excavate further, will we discover that the traditions, the customs and the beliefs across India may all be hand-me-downs from the Harappans, some 5,000 or more years ago?

Who knows, Rakhigarhi could be proof of a civilization that may not be lost at all, couldn't it?

And we could be the actual descendants of ancient Harappans, now spread all over the Indian subcontinent.

So, the mystery of what happened to the lost civilization may finally be answered.

It never died.

We are perhaps living proof of that.

The people of India and Pakistan may carry the same DNA as the Harappan people, they say.

Isn't that amazing?

Where is it located: Hisar district, Haryana
Timeframe of Settlement: 7000 (pre-Harappan) – 1900 BCE
Who discovered it and when: ASI in 1963

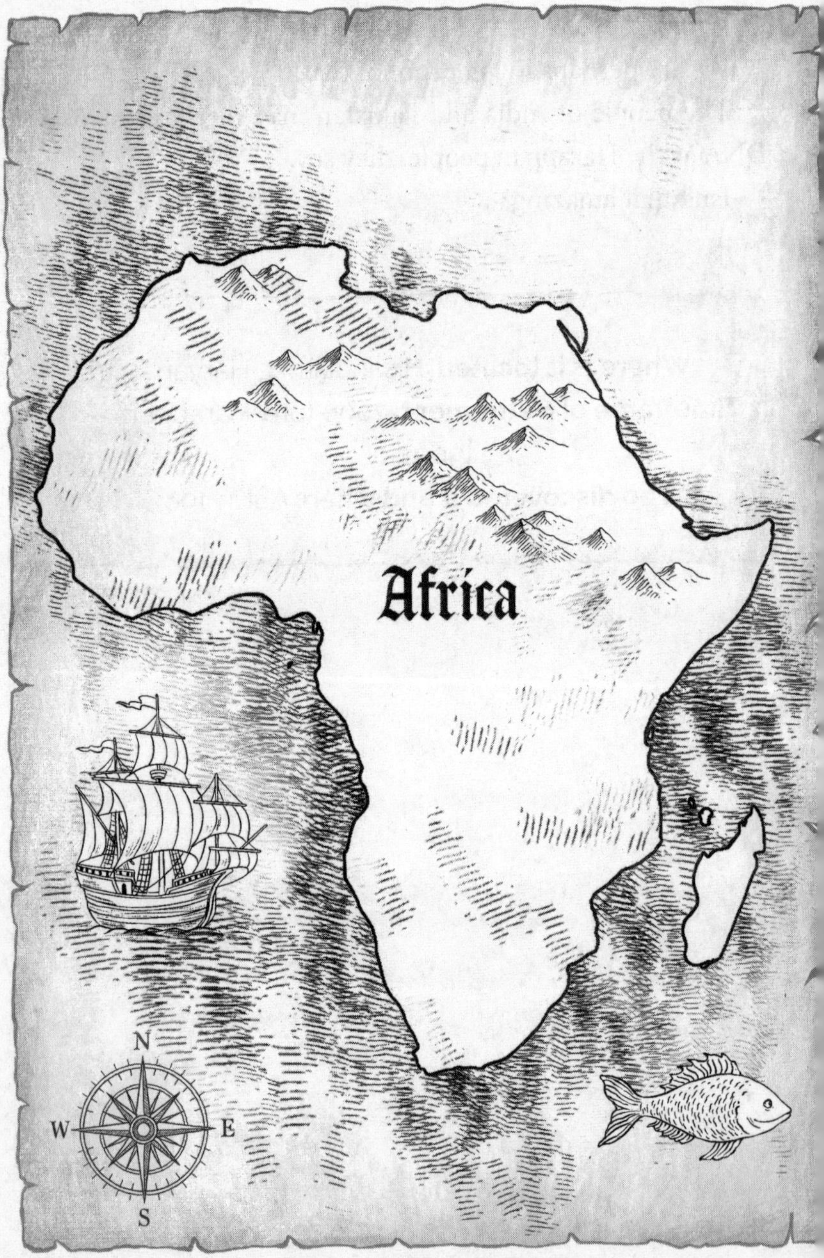
Africa
N
W
E
S

27

THONIS–HERACLEION

When the earth turns soft...

The sun was bright and the sky a clear blue.

It was a fine day for a reconnaissance flight, and the Royal Air Force Commander took off as usual.

Over the Mediterranean Sea and near the mouth of the River Nile, he flew.

Flying low, he spotted nothing unusual.

No lurking warships, no hidden submarines – not even the shadow of one.

However, something odd did catch his eagle eye.

So, he cruised even closer to the waters of Abu Qir Bay.

What did he see?

Under the ocean's shimmering, aquamarine waters, among the sand and darting fish were some strange shadows that oughtn't to have been there.

'What could it be?' he wondered.

Almost skimming the waves, he did a few more sorties.

Faint outlines of some stone blocks, columns, statues and maybe a few rock-like structures appeared.

'They look like some ancient ruins,' he thought.

Excited, he immediately alerted the authorities.

French archaeologist Franck Goddio and his team from the European Institute for Underwater Archaeology swiftly swung into action.

Scuba divers were promptly sent in; old maps and ancient texts were studied.

Hours were spent mapping and surveying the underwater structures and, to everyone's immense joy, the pilot's guess was right.

They were indeed ruins of an ancient lost settlement.

An ancient city, or cities, often mentioned in ancient Greek and Egyptian texts.

Cities that had long puzzled many historians, as they hadn't, until then, been able to find any places even remotely connected to those names.

So, they had concluded that they were mythical or legendary.

Now, however, sitting pretty underwater, where the River Nile joined the Mediterranean Sea, were not two cities, as they had once surmised from the texts, but one city with two names.

It was the city the Egyptians had called Thonis and the Greeks referred to as Heracleion.

The Greeks had apparently named it after their Greek hero, Heracles, who had built a great temple on the spot where he had first stepped on Egyptian soil.

The ruins of which temple, once winched up, were now on display for all to see and marvel at.

It was also the city to which Paris had first run away with the beautiful Helen of Troy – an act that had led to the famous Trojan War between the Trojans and the Greeks who wanted Helen back.

With 1,600 years of history behind it, Thonis-Heracleion had obviously been a popular and thriving port city at one time.

Now, evidently forgotten and unknown, it had lain hidden among the waters of the bay for over 1,000 years, until our eagle-eyed pilot happened to come along.

How had it so mysteriously vanished from sight?

What was the great mystery behind Thonis-Heracleion's disappearance into the sea?

Let's scroll back to sometime in the eighth century CE.

It was business as usual at Thonis-Heracleion.

Ships sailed in. Ships sailed out.

Some dropped anchor, some passed by.

Dock workers busily loaded, unloaded, stacked and stored.

Gold, silver, wine, oil and pottery passed through its portals.

Customs officials hurriedly stamped and forwarded cargo between ships.

The smell of spice and perfumed oil wafted through the air.

The blasts of ship horns echoed through the bay.

Nobody had any time to loiter or linger.

Controlling trade that came into Egypt from the Mediterranean, Thonis-Heracleion was a busy trading port.

However, it was a city built across many little islands of hard clay, silt, mudbanks and marshland, with a network of canals and harbours linked by bridges off the coast of Egypt.

A place that was prone to earthquakes, tsunamis and rising sea levels.

To top it all, it had several heavy stone wharves, many huge temples and towers.

So, as time went by, its foundations began to weaken, the soil gradually began to lose its firmness, and the port began to sink in parts.

Residents were known to flee, as the sea too had started to claim more and more of their land.

Then one day, Crete, a nearby country, was rocked by a massive earthquake, and in its aftermath, Thonis-Heracleion was hit by huge floods.

As busy as the vital trade hub was, without any warning, the town began to collapse.

Hapi, the massive, pink-granite god of fertility and prosperity, 16 feet tall and weighing 5,433 kg, who stood overlooking the bay, was the first to fall.

He tottered and he swayed as the soil under his feet slipped away.

Before he knew it, he was well on his way into a mud-soaked watery grave.

Then, one by one, like dominoes, the rest of Thonis-Heracleion fell.

The two massive temples of God Amun and his son, several enormous statues, great colonnades, mansions and then the market plazas disappeared into the bay.

"Egyptian god Hapi bearing offerings"

When clayey soil – from the silt sediment of the Nile – filled with moisture is shaken, it transforms from solid into fluid to become a swamp of quicksand that sinks anything that stands on it, especially a city like Thonis-Heracleion with its super-heavy, stone buildings.

It's called silt liquefaction, and it happens very fast.

Many lost their lives that day.

Unsung and unnoticed, they then lay in the Mediterranean Sea at the mouth of the river Nile, among the ruins of their once great city.

Now let's fast forward to sometime in 1996 CE: that's when Franck Goddio and his men came to Thonis-Heracleion's rescue.

They scoped out the seabed and then, with magnetometers, advanced sonar technology and teams of divers, confirmed that it was indeed Thonis-Heracleion, the once-greatest port on Earth.

Among other relics found, there were hieroglyphic inscriptions, 700 ship anchors, seventy shipwrecks, a baris cargo boat made of acacia wood and also a military ship.

While most of the lost city still lies silent underwater, although no longer lost, some of it has been excavated and brought up for everyone to admire.

And yes, our friend Hapi – the gigantic pink god – is also among them.

Lying around, as if patiently waiting to be rescued, is, however, the rest of Thonis-Heracleion.

Thus, it is today a popular diving spot.

How amazing it would be, wouldn't it, if we could also dive down and pick up relics of a shipwreck or two?

Where is it located: Abu Qir Bay, off the coast of Egypt

Timeframe of Settlement: Eighth century BCE–Eighth century CE

Who discovered it and when: Franck Goddio, European Institute for Underwater Archaeology in 2000

28

LOST CITY OF KALAHARI

When red sands hide secrets...

Its quiz time again.

It has one of the largest diamond mines in the world.

It has the largest number of game reserves in the world.

It runs for miles and miles through many countries.

Lions, meerkats, antelope, hyenas and cheetahs call it home.

It is a desert and yet not a desert.

What is it?

Was it easy to guess?

No?

Well, it is the Kalahari Desert in Africa, and it could well be hiding a few secrets.

Like a lost city perhaps, deep down below, in the bowels of its red sands.

A lost city that even SpaceX's CEO, Elon Musk's grandfather, went looking for.

The Kalahari Desert covers some 9,00,000 sq. km and goes through Botswana, Namibia and South Africa and is known for its beautiful uncut diamonds.

Rich in copper and uranium too, it is one of the most ancient deserts in the world and has perhaps been around for over sixty million years.

With its wide-open spaces and black-maned lions, it's a fascinating place.

Now, sometime in 1885, a magician-cum-explorer-cum-adventurer, William Hunt, also known as Farini, decided to go looking for diamonds in South Africa.

And he, along with a few companions, got completely lost in the Kalahari Desert.

So, while they floundered among the sand dunes, trying to get back to civilization, Farini came across what he thought were the ruins of a city.

'A "lost" city in the middle of a semi desert?' he marvelled. 'How could that be?'

So, he dug around further and among the rubble, of what he likened to the Great Wall of China after an earthquake, he found remnants of well-cut, square-shaped stones meshed together at right angles.

To him they seemed human-made.

He was convinced they were the ruins of a stone city or a hitherto unknown civilization now buried beneath the sands of the Kalahari.

When he returned, he published his findings and presented a paper before the Royal Geographical Society.

Although some disbelieved him, Hunt or Farini's presentations and findings caused a great stir in the Western world.

So, expedition after expedition set off to explore the Kalahari.

They rode in on camels, drove in on jeeps and even flew in on a light aircraft.

Some thirty or more such expeditions have, over the years, gone hoping to unearth Hunt's supposedly lost city.

A few have reported finding some brick-and-stone remains spread across the Kalahari that weren't natural formations and could be man-made.

However, no one has been able to come up with any conclusive proof that such a city, or what he thought was a city, truly existed.

Many renowned explorers believed that Hunt's claim may have been exaggerated.

Now, almost seventy-five years later, experts still hunting for Farini's lost civilization were able to roughly pinpoint the area of his lost city.

Yes, they said, Hunt's stone remnants had been found; however, they weren't human-made but a natural formation of dolerite rock, common to that area, that could be mistaken for a lost city.

Even so, explorers continue to haunt the Kalahari.

Elon Musk's grandfather, Joshua Norman Haldeman, went no fewer than twelve times hoping to find some clue.

He flew over the desert countless times, only to be disappointed.

However, it isn't as if settlements didn't thrive in the Kalahari.

They did.

Although the Kalahari, or *Kgalagadi* in the native dialect, means great thirst or a waterless place, it is a semi-desert with some dense vegetation and a river running through.

It is a semi-arid savanna that receives between 250–500 mm of rain each year.

The second largest desert in Africa after the Sahara, it has, for the last 20,000 years, been home to the San people, often referred to as the Bushmen of the Kalahari.

So, it isn't as if a city or a civilization couldn't have flourished or survived there.

In fact, buried beneath some dense vegetation in South Africa's Suikerbosrand Nature Reserve, the city of Kweneng, dating back to the fifteenth century, was discovered thanks to Google Earth and LiDAR technology.

However, so far, of Hunt or Farini's 'lost' city of the Kalahari there is no sign.

Who knows, with more modern technology it may only be a matter of time before it does turn up.

An exciting thought, isn't it?

Where is it located: Kalahari Desert, South Africa
Timeframe of Settlement: Unknown
Who discovered it and when: William Hunt in 1885

Meet the new tools on the block

A flat trowel is the most common tool that archaeologists use to dig.

However, humans with trowels and brushes, shovels, spades and, yes, dollops of patience may soon be a thing of the past with, who knows, robots, AI or Artificial Intelligence and Advanced Radar Systems – the new tools on the block – taking their place.

They will help you discover lost cities buried under desert sands or dense vegetation, map ancient trade routes that linked civilizations across the world and may soon even reveal identities of long-lost temples and palaces without messing up the ground.

LiDAR is a remote-sensing method with sensors and lasers placed on drones, planes or helicopters used to search and examine the surface of the Earth. It can discover and digitally map impenetrable ground and thick forests not visible to the human eye.

AI, an essential tool in uncovering our past, is used to quickly analyse and improve the data collected by LiDAR sensors to identify patterns and predict obstacles. It can also decipher ancient texts and analyse satellite images.
E.g. Chinese scientists discovered an ancient language found on turtle shells and ox bones. AI was able to classify the bone structure and piece together the fragments that had inscriptions of Chinese – earliest recorded history.

Google Earth can remotely identify archaeological sites. It compiles images from various sources, from photos taken by orbiting satellites or planes, kites, drones and even balloons thousands of kilometres above Earth or even closer.
E.g. Google Earth was used to identify hundreds of archaeological sites in Saudi Arabia and Yemen.

Synthetic Aperture Radar (SAR) penetrates vegetation, ice and sand easily to detect any structures hiding within or below. It uses radar signals to map underground structures and find buried buildings without excavation. You can now see through layers of sand to create high-resolution images of structures below the surface.

SAR recently discovered a 5,000-year-old lost civilization buried in the Rub' al Khali (Empty Quarter) beneath the so-far impenetrable Dubai desert.

Genomics uses genetic fingerprinting or DNA profiling traces the origin of any animal , man or thing even if remains are found continents away. For example through DNA samples, walrus ivory from medieval Europe could be traced back to walruses from Greenland's Arctic waters.

And don't forget the **Mitochondrial Eve**: Mitochondrial DNA (mtDNA), genetic material found in human cells, suggests that all living humans have descended through their mother's line from a single woman who lived in the middle of the Kalahari Desert in Africa between 2,00,000 and 3,00,000 years ago.

Europe
N
W
E
S

29

POMPEII

When mountains erupt...

Have you heard of Pompeii?

The port city on the lower slopes of Mount Vesuvius in Italy, off the coast of the Mediterranean Sea?

You haven't?

Well, that isn't surprising.

It has been covered in a blanket of ash and rock for at least 2,000 years.

However, if you have, then you must know it is that ancient Roman city that archaeologists have – over the past few centuries – been uncovering bit by bit, building by building.

Even as recently as June of 2024, archaeologists have unearthed a remarkably well-preserved blue room with frescoes of lovely women.

It was found among the ruins of what must have once been a sophisticated, prosperous city bustling with life.

Why do we think that?

Well, because many beautiful buildings had already been excavated from around the same site.

Just imagine, it actually included an ornate banquet hall with frescoes depicting fully laden tables of fruit and meat intact.

And long before that as well, sometime in the sixteenth century, Domenico Fontana, an architect from nearby Naples, while digging around in the suburbs of Torre Annunziata, stumbled upon a wall complete with exquisite paintings and detailed inscriptions.

It was he who first guessed that an entire city may well have been lost and buried under all that rock and mud.

And he was right.

Since then, periodic excavations have happened, throwing up more and more proof of a well-developed, ancient town that had been unknown to the rest of the world. And guess what?

It also included a wall inscription that referred to the place as, 'Pompeii'.

So, what happened to Pompeii? Where did its people go?

The answer to that is in some first-century letters written by a Roman gentleman called Pliny the Younger.

They shed some interesting light on what happened.

Some 2,000 years ago, it had, as usual, been a fine morning in Pompeii.

Holidaymakers made merry on its beaches and shoppers thronged its markets.

It was a city bustling with life.

Suddenly, a thunderous boom resounded through the air.

The ground shook violently and buildings started to sway.

Stalls around the market square collapsed and people stumbled.

Now, Pompeii was often prone to earthquakes.

Seventeen years earlier, a massive one had shaken it to its core.

So, was it another earthquake? The people wondered worriedly.

However, it was much worse than that.

Mount Vesuvius, the volatile volcano nearby, had erupted.

Spewing smoke and poisonous gases miles into the air above, it emitted clouds of hot ash and pumice that began to rain down.

Alarmed, the butcher hastily shut shop.

The baker stopped baking, and the candlestick-maker began packing his wares.

Everyone made a panic-stricken beeline for the seven exit gates of the city.

'Get to the sea, get to the water!' was the cry.

Many managed to escape. Many didn't. Many couldn't.

A zillion tons of fine, soft, hot ash began to pile up.

Ten feet deep and more, it blocked doorways and windows.

"The Last Day of Pompeii, *painting by Karl Bryullov (1830–1833)*"

Roofs caved in and walls crumbled under its weight.

On the streets and within their houses, unable to breathe, people froze where they stood or fell.

Then, worst of all, a flood of lava and molten rocks in glowing waves of what scientists call a pyroclastic surge, hurtled down at a deadly speed, scorching everything in its path.

And two days later, when the shaking and the eruption finally ended, Pompeii, the once-thriving port in ancient Rome, was history.

It was as if the celebrated city of about 160–170 acres had never existed.

Along with more than half its 20,000 residents, Pompeii, with its elegant temples and villas, had, almost overnight, disappeared under a blanket of ash and rock, 20-30 feet deep.

So had Herculaneum, another city nearby.

The year: 79 CE.

And how do we know this?

Pliny the Younger, remember him?

He witnessed it and wrote about it twenty-five years later.

His uncle, a naval admiral of the fleet, had died in that eruption.

For the next 1,700 years, Pompeii lay thus buried.

Its landscape completely obliterated, and with no one alive, Pompeii gradually faded from memory.

Those who had escaped settled elsewhere in nearby towns or far away – and in time, were also soon long gone.

Eventually, its name became part of ancient lore and its location forgotten.

Apart from a few artefacts or a mosaic or two that would pop up every now and then, arid and deserted, the city was lost to the world.

And even though efforts like those of the sixteenth-century architect threw up clues, no systematic excavations really took place.

Finally, in the eighteenth century, while digging nearby to lay the foundation for a summer palace, remnants of a few elegant villas popped up and intrigued the then King of Naples.

So, excavations began in earnest.

And in the next 300 years or so, as they gradually cleared most of the dirt and rubble, the ruins of a grand sea-trading resort emerged, almost intact.

Archaeologists were amazed to find that underneath all the debris, Pompeii appeared to be exactly as it had been some 2,000 years ago.

How was that?

One archaeologist, Giuseppe Fiorelli, found that the imprints on the ashes of everything, especially of those that had decomposed or carbonized, had formed cavities.

So, he hit upon a brilliant idea.

He made tiny holes in the ground and carefully poured plaster through them.

When the plaster set, he carefully excavated whatever was inside.

And what emerged was extraordinary.

Among other incredible things, casts of a couple hiding in a bedroom clutching their gold and silver; a man trying to escape through a window; a dog struggling to breathe; a gladiator holding his helmet – all dead but frozen and preserved to the last detail and expression.

The layers of ash had helped preserve everything – its streets, buildings, villas, amphitheatres, vineyards, paintings, sculptures and even the shapes of the bodies of those people and animals buried alive.

And like that highly decorated banquet hall, with frescoes of tables of food intact, there were also bakeries with loaves still in the ovens and cooking pots with half-done duck, goat, pig and fish, in what must have been their kitchens.

A large, four-wheeled ceremonial chariot with the remains of harnessed horses was also found.

Also among the ashes was an ivory figure of Mahalakshmi – the Hindu goddess of wealth.

So, Pompeii must have been a place where wealthy Romans visited or lived, where even as early as the first century, there was interaction between ancient India and ancient Rome.

Although only two thirds – 109 acres – of Pompeii has been excavated so far, we now know what life must have been like for the ancient Romans.

Today, rediscovered Pompeii is a popular tourist spot and a UNESCO World Heritage Site.

Scholars, students and eager travellers flock to admire the well-preserved ruins and sculptures, and to gaze at Mount Vesuvius and wonder whether it will erupt again.

Who knows, it might, say scientists, so be prepared.

Where is it located: Bay of Naples, Italy, south of present-day Naples.

Timeframe of Settlement: Seventh century BCE–79 CE

Who discovered it and when: Architect Domenico Fontana in 1592

30

SKARA BRAE

When sand dunes clear...

Have you ever wondered what it might have been like to live in a prehistoric age?

Let's take the first of the prehistoric ages – the Palaeolithic Age or Old Stone Age – when man lived in caves and moved from place-to-place hunting for food.

An Age which lasted a mind-boggling 2,00,000 to 10,000 BCE or so.

An Age that gradually gave way to the Mesolithic Age or Middle Stone Age, which was only marginally better, and then into another called the Neolithic Age or the New Stone Age – 9000 to 4500 BCE – when man no longer led a nomadic life.

Instead, he began to gradually settle down in one place, grew crops, domesticated animals and lived off the same patch of land.

It was a simple life that took care of all his basic needs – food, water and shelter.

He probably wore skins and fashioned tools out of polished stone.

Then, as centuries flew by, man evolved and developed through many other ages like the Bronze and Iron Ages, to finally arrive at our present stage in life, the Industrial or Modern Age where we want for nothing.

We don't, do we?

We get just about everything before we even think of it, and with a touch of our fingertips we can even send a man into space or the moon.

Well, all right, now for a moment, let's go back to the prehistoric age.

Not so long ago, about 200 years ago, perhaps during your great-grandparents' time, there was, in Scotland, in the Orkney Islands, a mighty storm.

The wind howled incessantly, massive thunder and lightning split the skies.

The waves rose high and battered the shore ferociously for days and it seemed as if the sky gods were angry.

When the storm finally subsided, the land was left barren and bare.

The sand dunes that dotted the shores were completely stripped of their sand, too.

And what got left behind was an underground village of sorts.

Standing exposed to the sun was a cluster of roofless stone houses.

Circular huts built of stone, some four of them, interconnected by passages and doorways.

Even the furniture was stone – beds, shelves, cupboards, tables and chairs.

The experts were promptly summoned.

Radiocarbon dating of the layers of soil, to everyone's shock, pegged it to be at least 5,000 years old.

It was a prehistoric village built and occupied between 3000 BCE and 2500 BCE during – wait for it – the Neolithic Age.

So perfectly preserved despite its age, it stunned the world.

What was amazing was that it had lain thus hidden and undisturbed for centuries and centuries under those dunes.

Soon, archaeologists dug up another four houses when, a few years later, another storm exposed even more huts and artefacts.

Jewellery, pottery, beads, buttons and dice made of bone and teeth were found.

The recovered bones, polished stone tools and remains of barley and wheat told us that they might have been fishermen and farmers.

Sheep-horn tools and utensils of sheepskin remnants found, indicated that they probably reared sheep – and probably cattle and pigs too.

So, could it have been a settlement of sheep farmers as well?

Maybe. They could even have been the United Kingdom's very first farmers.

Behind Skara Brae is the Loch of Skaill, a freshwater lake filled with fish and eel.

So, perhaps Britain's first fishermen too.

They seemed to have lived close to each other in houses that were similar.

Each had a door that was secured with a wooden or whale-bone bar across it.

New houses also appear to have been built over old foundations.

Now began the quest to find out more about this buried city and how it was lost.

So, the locals nearby began uncovering it bit by bit.

All in all, about eight houses were excavated from under a large mound known to the locals simply as 'Skerrabra'.

'Skerrabra' with time, got turned into Skara, nobody knew what that meant but *Brae* they knew meant 'hill'.

And so, the lost city of Skara Brae was thus born.

It appeared to have been part of a large settlement.

Was it abandoned suddenly?

Yes, say some historians, seeing the manner in which artefacts and meat joints were strewn across the huts.

A violent sandstorm – perhaps like the one 200 years ago – may have forced them to flee with nothing but their lives, leaving behind their belongings in haste.

No, say other historians.

It was a gradual desertion.

Due to constant storms and tidal waves people may have moved away to safer places.

However, it was so long ago that it is difficult to say what really happened.

Carbon dating of the organic remains that have been excavated tells us it's likely that Skara Brae was perhaps occupied for about 600 years and finally abandoned around 2500 BCE.

Its remnants covered and preserved by sand for thousands of years, now exposed, bore witness to their lives and story.

A story that was lost to us for eons due to a natural calamity or climate change but nevertheless preserved and revealed by the same natural forces.

It is today, a UNESCO World Heritage Site.

So, just imagine – we now know how people in the Neolithic Age in the UK lived, what they ate, where they stayed and what they did.

How remarkable is that!

Where is it located: On the Bay of Skaill in the parish of Sandwick, Orkney Islands, Scotland

Timeframe of Settlement: 3000 BCE–2500 BCE

Who discovered it and when:

William Watt (a local landowner and laird of Skaill) in 1850;

Gordon Childe in the 1920s

31

PAVLOPETRI

When oceans hide secrets...

There were hundreds of people.

The police had a difficult time marshalling them.

On the beach and in the water, they stood.

Linking hands, they attempted to form a symbolic human chain.

Citizens from the Greek islands of Neapolis and Elafonisos, they were determined to make a point.

And what was their point?

'Save Pavlopetri! Protect Pavlopetri!' was their demand.

So, what was this mysterious Pavlopetri?

And why did it need saving?

From whom did it need protection?

To find out, we need to go back a little in history.

In 1967, Nicholas Flemming, a marine geo-archaeologist from the Institute of Oceanography, Southampton University, went for a swim.

He had heard rumours of a lost city just off the southern coast of mainland Greece.

So that day, he decided to dive into the waters that lay next to a sandy beach on Vatika Bay in south-eastern Peloponnese, off the Laconian coast.

As he dived, he first spotted some old tombs that certainly didn't look like any lost city.

So, he swam back towards the mainland.

And there he struck gold.

He found mysterious rock foundations of what looked like houses.

To his immense joy, the seabed was covered with many such uncut stone foundations.

Thrilled, he came up for air, and then made drawings of what he had discovered and sent them off to the university.

Soon, a team of archaeological divers from Cambridge University came to survey and vet the scene.

What they discovered was every archaeologist's dream.

Lying just a few metres below the surface of the sea was a perfect blueprint of a well-laid city, a layout of fifteen dwellings of stone and mudbrick in grid fashion, courtyards, streets, chamber tombs and at least thirty-seven graves.

Interspersed with many recovered shards of Greek pottery, urns and jugs were foreign artefacts as well.

The artefacts recovered were mostly intact and discernible, but seemed to be very old, almost as ancient as the Bronze Age.

That thrilled the marine archaeologists.

Their excitement spiralled when some pieces from the Neolithic Age also showed up.

Wouldn't that make Flemming's discovery at least 5,000 years old?

Yes, it would.

And perhaps among the oldest underwater ruins in the world.

It also meant that the historians had discovered none other than the lost city of Pavlopetri, meaning Paul's Stone, named after Peter and Paul, the two apostles of Christ.

It had been a bustling port in the Christian era.

Nobody, however, knew if it was known by any other name earlier. Cloth must've been produced on a mass scale, for export perhaps, as circular stones used as weights to hold threads in place in looms lay around in plenty too.

Pavlopetri thus, between 3000 BCE and 1100 BCE, must've been a popular port where ships plied to and fro, carrying textile and other goods up and down to various countries.

Now, the well-laid layout was well preserved, but the houses were not.

The walls of the houses appeared damaged by ships that still plied that route and dropped anchor without realizing what lay below.

Also, the discharge of waste, ballast water and cleaning chemicals from large ships anchored nearby, was polluting the waters of the bay as well as the ruins.

Plus, there was danger of damage from a natural-gas pipeline and a power plant nearby.

Earlier, in 1904, geologist and president of the Academy of Athens, Fokion Negris, had spoken of some ruins in the seabed near Elafonisos.

However, neither he nor anybody else had followed it up, until Flemming decided to go for a dive and swim that day.

As soon as the news of the discovery of the lost harbour city spread, amateur archaeologists began to haunt the scene.

So did excited souvenir hunters.

With no security in place, Pavlopetri soon became a looter's paradise.

Casual snorkelers and scuba divers dived down to look for relics – and carry them home as mementoes.

Relics that could have given archaeologists more information were simply taken away.

Thus, between constructions that were coming up along the coast, large ships still plying the same waters and souvenir hunters, the Pavlopetri remains were in danger of being completely lost or destroyed.

And that is why people from the neighbouring islands congregated that day – to hold a protest.

They wanted the authorities to save the archaeological remains of the underwater port of Pavlopetri and protect it from these dangers.

The authorities complied.

Buoys were placed in the water to mark out the area where the ancient sunken city lay submerged.

Spread over more than 80,000 sq. m, it was a large expanse.

The Greek navy has also listed the area on marine charts so that ships may avoid the area.

However, it lies close to the surface – no more than one to four metres – and it's too difficult to prevent determined pilferers and enthusiastic swimmers from exploring.

This small underwater islet of Pavlopetri – one of the oldest sunken cities in the world – is our heritage, say the Greeks, and needs to be saved.

They hope to get the authorities to set up rules to regulate or prevent the passage of large ships and small, create public awareness and protect the site.

Thus, since 2016, it has been placed on the World Monuments Watch, that has been celebrated every year thereon.

Thanks to Flemming, one of the world's oldest sunken ports and cities is no longer lost and forgotten.

So, how was it 'lost' in the first place?

Three massive earthquakes between 1000 BCE and 375 CE may have slowly but surely submerged the city from which it couldn't emerge, say scholars.

It had then lain undisturbed and frozen in time for more than 3,000 years under the sea.

With photographs, maps and measurements of the underwater Pavlopetri ruins, they are now able to predict the location and speed of earthquake movements and any changes in global sea level that may have happened.

Hence, they hope to unravel ancient Pavlopetri's still mystifying loss from world memory, bit by bit.

In the meantime, if you are up for a bit of organized snorkelling and ruin-gazing, Pavlopetri beckons.

There are underwater signs and routes to guide you.

So, if it's a dive you want – go for it, you won't get lost.

Where is it located: South-eastern Laconian coast, on the Bay of Vatika, Peloponnese, Greece

Timeframe of Settlement: 3000 BCE–1000 BCE

Who discovered it and when:

Nicholas Flemming, of the Institute of Oceanography, University of Southampton in 1967

32

TROY

When myths turn into reality...

Henrich Schliemann was seven years old when he first heard of Troy.

He saw a picture of Troy in a book his father gave him for Christmas.

Troy had been a prosperous city near the Dardanelles Straits, that connected the Aegean Sea to the Black Sea.

An important fortified Mediterranean port, it had, however, long disappeared from history and the map of the world, if it ever was there at all.

The book, *World History for Children,* carried illustrations of the city of Troy burning – and young Schliemann was fascinated by it.

Now, the city of Troy was famous.

It figured prominently in another book too – *Iliad*, the famous Greek classic from the eighth century BCE.

Written by the blind Greek poet Homer, it narrated the story of the Trojan War.

A war that started after Paris, a prince of Troy, abducted Helen, the beautiful wife of Menelaus, King of Sparta, and brought her home to Troy.

Now Menelaus couldn't allow that, could he?

So, he rallied other kingdoms around him and with all his Greek allies, set sail for Troy to rescue her.

However, if Menelaus thought it would be easy to retrieve his queen, he was in for a surprise.

If he had brave warriors like Achilles and Patroclus known for their military prowess, so did Troy.

" Achilles tending Patroclus wounded by an arrow "

Paris's brother, Hector, was an equally brilliant warrior if not better and he, with his men, held Menelaus and his allies off for ten long years.

It was a bloody siege.

However, both sides were evenly matched.

Until the Greeks tricked the Trojans.

The Greeks cunningly concealed their soldiers inside a humungous wooden horse, abandoned it at the gates of Troy and pretended to sail away.

Believing the Greeks had accepted defeat and withdrawn, the Trojans gleefully trundled the wooden horse into their city – unaware of the enemy soldiers hidden within.

Once inside the gates of Troy, the Greek soldiers waited, then at midnight clambered out, took the Trojans by surprise and massacred them.

And then set Troy on fire.

After that, there was no way Troy could recover.

Now, the story of Troy had long been considered a myth, perhaps an invention of Homer's vivid imagination.

Over time, no one knew whether it had happened or not, or even whether Troy as a city had existed at all.

Young Schliemann, however, continued to be intrigued by it.

The pictures of Troy burning sparked his imagination and captivated him.

Could the Trojan War have really happened, he wondered?

Was there actually a city called Troy?

He was determined to find out.

Schliemann became a Homer fan.

A gifted child, he learnt all there was to know about Homer and his poems and, by the time he was a young man, had not only learnt to speak Greek but had made himself a fortune as well.

You see, he needed the money to chase his dream.

And his dream?

No guesses – to find the *Iliad*'s city of Troy and see if it existed.

And in 1873, he did just that, with help from Frank Calvert, a British diplomat, whose family owned some land in present-day Türkiye.

It was in a place called Hisarlık, that boasted of a huge mound, 65 feet high.

It was around the ruins of an old Greek/Roman city called Ilium where, according to long-held belief, Troy was suspected to have been.

So off he went to Hisarlık, and with Calvert's help began excavating the mound.

There, to his delight, he uncovered the remains of a walled citadel, a fortress and other artefacts.

However, Schliemann soon found that there were many settlements stacked one below the other at the site.

As he dug deeper into the dirt and rock, he found layer after layer of a city built at different times.

So, every time the city burned down or was destroyed – maybe by fire or earthquakes – the people, after a period of time, simply built their new homes or cities over the old remains.

There were thus remnants of nine layers – so nine different Troys.

The nine layers represented nine periods of time during which Troy was destroyed and rebuilt.

And so, the archaeologists marked them in Roman numerals, I–IX, from bottom upwards – the oldest being right at the bottom.

Now, Schliemann was no trained archaeologist.

So, in his enthusiasm, he was careless.

When, at layer II – which was almost at the bottom – he found what he excitedly thought were remnants of his Troy, he inadvertently damaged a lot of the remains of the Troys above.

He was not to know that layer II was of an even older Troy than Homer's.

He also collected a lot of treasure from the site and proclaimed it to be 'Priam's treasure'.

Priam was Paris and Hector's father, and the king of Troy during the Trojan War.

That claim, however, has been declared doubtful by other archaeologists and historians, as Schliemann was known to exaggerate.

Nevertheless, his findings caused a sensation, and he was hailed as a hero for discovering Homer's Troy.

A portrait of Heinrich Schliemann

Schliemann died soon after, believing he had indeed found Troy.

He had.

There was no doubt the mound was the site of the city of Troy, and it was he who had discovered what lay beneath it.

However, the layer he identified was not the actual level at which Homer's Troy lay.

He had dug through it.

Two other archaeologists, Wilhelm Dörpfeld and Carl Blegen, continued the investigation.

They used more advanced scientific methods and went about it more methodically than Schliemann to conclude that Homer's Troy didn't lie at level II.

While Dörpfeld believed it was at level VI, Blegen later proved it was neither, but that it actually lay at level VII-a.

And how did he conclude that?

He found more definitive evidence of a war and fire at VII-a than in Dörpfeld's layer.

He found arrowheads and marks of war embedded in the walls, unburied human skeletons, animal bones and burnt buildings – all of which led him to believe that this was the Troy destroyed in battle.

It also matched the period of the war mentioned in the *Iliad* and was probably razed to the ground by a devastating fire between 1260 BCE and 1240 BCE.

The layers above it pointed to a city called Ilium, which was another name for Troy in later years.

Thereafter, buried under its own debris, it too had faded from memory.

And thus, ancient Troy, for 4,000 years, had remained a part of the *Iliad* – a mythical city, a poet's imagination or perhaps even a fantasy.

It had even spawned many plays, TV shows, books, documentaries and grand movies as a Greek legendary story.

So, a myth or a legend, something that has long baffled historians, thanks to Schliemann and his archaeologist friends, had now been proved real.

Today it's a popular UNESCO World Heritage Site.

As more and more lost cities are discovered, legends and myths are no longer found to be mere imaginary tales or ancient folklore but realities.

Isn't that cool?

Where is it located: Northwest coast of Anatolia in modern-day Turkey

Timeframe of settlement: 3600 BCE–1240 BCE

Who found it and when:

Heinrich Schliemann and Frank Calvert between 1871–1873;

Wilhelm Dörpfeld between 1893–1894;

Carl Blegen between 1932–1938;

Manfred Korfmann between 1988–2005

33

ATLANTIS

When imagination and fiction mingle...

Everybody likes a mystery.

You do too, don't you?

If so, here's one for you.

Long, long ago in the Greece of fourth century BCE, there lived a great philosopher.

His name was Plato, and he wrote some marvellous books.

Among them were two interconnected works on the dialogues of Timaeus and Critias.

These dialogues were conversations between Greek philosophers – Socrates, Hermocrates, Timaeus and Critias.

And in these books, these men talk about a super ideal kingdom.

'There was, my grandfather told me,' said Critias, 'some 9,000 years ago, a mighty powerful island kingdom, larger than Libya and Asia Minor put together. It was located in the Atlantic Ocean, just beyond the Pillars of Hercules. And it was called Atlantis.'

He then goes on to describe Atlantis and tell its story.

It was supposedly a prosperous and rich kingdom, advanced in every way.

Its king was powerful but just, and ruled over many lands throughout the Mediterranean, Africa and Europe.

It was a powerful empire known not only for its beauty and wealth but also for its wisdom and military strength.

Built in concentric circles of land and water, it was interconnected by tunnels and canals through which ships could ply.

Its lands were fertile and its buildings of red-and-black stone, stunningly beautiful.

With a well-laid-out irrigation system, its crops were plentiful.

Its citizens, wise, intelligent and handsome, were half-man and half-god.

Laws were implemented and rules observed.

Protected by the god Poseidon and guarded by large metal gates and tall towers, it was a powerful yet peaceful empire with happy people interested in knowledge and learning.

However, since all good times usually come to an end, so they did for Atlantis as well.

Its knowledge and power soon went to its head.

Its people changed. So did its king.

Pride and conceit took over.

They became, haughty, arrogant, cruel, wicked and impious.

Corruption became a way of life.

Atlantis waged unprovoked wars with other kingdoms within its realm and outside.

With every victory its arrogance grew.

Its citizens were no longer humble or kind but filled with sinful pride and ego.

Then Atlantis attacked Athens, a small nation.

And to her shock, Atlantis was roundly defeated.

Atlantis was not only defeated, but it was also humiliated and disgraced.

It lost control of most of its occupied territories.

Then nature decided to step in and complete its destruction.

The earth shook violently, and as the oceans arose, the earth opened up and wicked Atlantis was gone.

In a single day, Atlantis quite simply disappeared forever into the sea and the earth without a trace.

And ever since, the world has been engaged in a search for this mysterious city.

Now, west of the Strait of Gibraltar, off the Atlantic Sea, is where, according to his description, Plato's Atlantis lay.

So, every adventurer, explorer and archaeologist has, for centuries, been on its trail, but so far to no avail.

No sign of any such kingdom described by Plato has ever surfaced.

Modern sonar technology has also not revealed any kind of land mass on the Atlantic seabed, where it is supposed to have sunk.

Famous intellectuals, scientists and historians then came up with many theories.

Some pooh-poohed it as a mere allegory or a fictional narrative or fable created by Plato to make a point.

Plato, they believed, was trying to tell us what would happen when people turn arrogant and sinful.

There were others, however, who believed Atlantis did exist.

It could be Santorini (a Greek island) or near Scandinavia, or the Canary Islands or even America, they said.

Could it not be the continent of Antarctica or even Mars, they wondered.

After all, Antarctica does have a fascinating and mysterious seabed filled with an amazing underwater landscape of peaks and ravines.

As for Mars – well that does seem a little far-fetched, doesn't it?

Anyway, there was nothing so far to show that it was on either.

So, how did it vanish?

If it did exist, where could it have disappeared to?

All we have is Plato's word that Atlantis existed.

There's nothing else to prove its existence.

So, was Atlantis then a fictional place made up by Plato – a mere figment of his imagination?

Now at the time that Plato said Atlantis vanished, a devastating earthquake does appear to have taken place on Thera (Santorini) that destroyed a flourishing civilization on Crete, located near where Atlantis may have been.

So, if Atlantis was not Plato's invention, could it have been that Atlantis was destroyed?

Although so far untraceable, could it have disappeared into the sea or the earth at that time?

So, explorers, voyagers and treasure seekers to this day, fascinated by the thought of a missing Atlantis, continue to search for it under every sea, ocean and desert.

Yet, the question is, could a kingdom so wonderful really remain missing for so long?

Wouldn't someone have found some evidence of it somewhere if it really did exist?

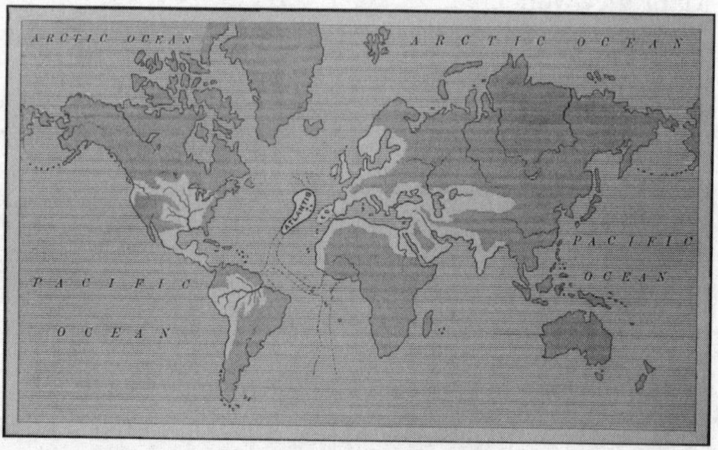

"A map showing the supposed extent of the Atlantean Empire, from Ignatius L. Donnelly's Atlantis: the Antediluvian World, 1882"

So then, could it be, as some believe, Plato trying to tell us what would happen to us if we became conceited and arrogant?

Sinful pride would lead to a fall even for the mightiest of mighty empires too.

No one, however, knows for sure.

And the lost city of Atlantis still continues to fascinate, puzzle and intrigue the world.

So, what do you think?

Could there be an actual Atlantis that's gone missing?

Or is it a myth, a legend – a totally fictional, made-up place?

A place that exists only within the pages of Plato's books?

You decide.

Where is it located: Atlantic Ocean the Straits of Gibraltar (that is, just beyond the Pillars of Hercules)

Timeframe of Settlement: Unknown

Who discovered it and when: No one to date

Oceania
N
W
E
S

34

ZEALANDIA

When continents submerge...

The Gods be gracious unto us even from the place whence Vishnu strode
Through the seven regions of the earth,
Through all this world strode Vishnu;
thrice his foot he planted, and the whole
Was gathered in his footsteps' dust...

(Rigveda, Book 1, Hymn 22, Verses 16–18)

Could the seven regions walked by Lord Vishnu be the seven continents of Asia, Africa, North America, South America, Antarctica, Europe and Australia – the continents our scientists and explorers have geographically divided the world into?

Well, if myth turns into reality, as has been happening so often, it must be.

Aha! but they didn't know at that time, did they, that there was going to be an eighth continent?

Yes, imagine, an eighth continent discovered as recently as 2017.

And it's called Zealandia.

Remember the ancient supercontinent Gondwana that was formed 550 million years ago?

The same Gondwana – Jurassic Period – from where places like South America, Africa, Arabia, Madagascar, India, Australia and Antarctica broke away and formed?

Apparently, so did this continent.

Located to the east of Australia, it was no small fragment, but it lay hidden and submerged underwater for millions of years.

It is a vast continent of some 4.9 million sq. km and its separation from Gondwana must have also happened between 60–100 million years ago.

While 94 per cent of it is underwater, the rest of the land that isn't is known as – can you guess what?

Yes, it's New Zealand along with two other islands – the French island of New Caledonia and the tiny Australian territories of Lord Howe Island and Ball's Pyramid.

And that is why American geophysicist Bruce Luyendyk in 1995 named the new continent – Zealandia, a take-off on New Zealand.

It is otherwise known as *Te Riu-a-Māui* in Māori, meaning 'hidden continent', as it is mostly submerged.

Both names seem apt, don't you think?

Well, since it is still almost entirely underwater, Lord Vishnu and our ancient mariners perhaps cannot yet be held to account – or proven wrong either – can they?

So, how did all the other continents get their names?

Interestingly, they're mostly derived from Greek words and names of European explorers decided by mapmakers.

America was named not after Christopher Columbus, who believed he had landed in India, but after a sixteenth-century Italian explorer, Amerigo Vespucci, who arrived in America soon after him and realized there were two separate land masses. So, thanks to German cartographers Martin Waldseemüller and Gerardus Mercator, they became the continents of North and South America.

Antarctica came from the Greek word *antarktikos*, meaning 'opposite of the Arctic', referring to 'far north', and was first used by Marinus of Tyre, a Greek-speaking Roman mapmaker.

Africa, the second largest continent, originally referred to as 'Alkebulan', was perhaps – but nobody knows for sure – later named after a tribe called Afri by the Romans, meaning 'the land of the Afri'.

Now, Asia – the largest continent – could've come from the ancient Greek word *Ἀσία*,' that the Greek historian and traveller, Herodotus, coined.

Australia, the smallest, was derived from the Latin word *australis*, which means, 'southern', popularized first by a nineteenth-century explorer, Matthew Flinders.

And charmingly, Europe was probably named after a mythical Greek princess named Europa, daughter of Zeus.

Fascinatingly simple, isn't it?

However, while all these other continents are comprised of many countries, Zealandia has just three – New Zealand and the two islands.

With only 6 per cent of land jutting out, submerged Zealandia is almost as large as Australia, is funnily shaped and may have separated from Australia about 80 million years ago.

Lying just 2 km below the surface of the South Pacific Ocean, it's the smallest, thinnest and youngest continent in the world.

For the first time ever, experts today, thanks to satellite imaging and modern technology, have been able to completely map it underwater.

Now, we know 71 per cent of our planet is covered by the waters of the five oceans – Atlantic, Pacific, Indian, Arctic and the Southern.

The remaining 29 per cent is land that makes up the seven continents, which means Zealandia, under the blue waters of the South Pacific Ocean, was hidden in plain sight, just waiting for us to discover it.

And it was, but not as easily as the others.

As early as 1642, a seafaring Dutch explorer named Abel Tasman first sailed up to what was to become New Zealand.

Chased off by its indigenous people – the Māoris – he went back home and declared to the world that there was a new southern land mass to be explored.

“ *Landing of Lieutenant James Cook at Botany Bay in 1770, painting by E. Phillips Fox* ”

This new land mass was then named after a Dutch province called Zeeland by Dutch mapmakers as 'Nova Zeelandia', which later turned into the now-anglicized 'New Zealand'.

It, however, took another 100-odd years before the British explorer Captain James Cook went looking for New Zealand.

While Australia was already known, he was the first European to set foot on and then map New Zealand on behalf of the British Crown.

However, neither Cook nor anybody else perhaps thought to look at what lay submerged off the coast of New Zealand or Australia.

Another 100-odd years were to pass before a Scottish naturalist, Sir James Hector, in 1875, went on a survey of New Zealand's southern coast.

He was the first to wonder if there was indeed a hidden land mass underwater.

Again, nothing happened for a long while.

Then, in the 1960s, interest revived when geologists began to discover more compelling evidence underwater.

About five decades later, scientific expeditions could confirm the presence of earthly rock formations, a significant amount of crust as in any continent and, importantly, yes, a large area of land.

When they discovered the kind of granite and limestone found on land, unlike the ocean floor, which is mostly full of igneous rocks like basalt, they were sure.

Thus, in 2017, imagine, almost 375 years after it was first noticed, experts finally and officially recognized Zealandia as a microcontinent.

So, was Zealandia ever above water at any time?

Who or what used to live there? And how long has it now been underwater?

Was New Zealand also perhaps once submerged?

All questions experts are still trying to fathom out.

Unable to collect fossils directly from its seabed, scientists are drilling deep down to uncover more details from seabed rock samples of the newly minted continent.

Dinosaurs, allosaurs and giant elephant birds are known to have roamed Gondwana.

So also New Zealand.

Who knows, we may perhaps soon find remnants of their relatives hidden in the deep blue of Zealandia's heart as well.

Now, what could be more exciting than that?

Where is it located: South Pacific Ocean

Timeframe of Settlement: 100-60 million years ago

Who discovered it and when:

Scottish naturalist Sir James Hector in 1875

ARCHAEOLOGICAL NUGGETS

1. The King of Babylon, Nabonidus – sixth century BCE, was the world's first archaeologist. He dug up the thousands-of-years-old Ebabbar temple floor in Sippar – in today's Iraq – to check its foundations and reconstruct it.
2. The Sumerian civilization of Mesopotamia – 3100 BCE, is among the oldest civilization on the planet.
3. Jéricho, West Bank, Palestine, dating back around 11,000 years, is one of the oldest cities in the world. It has about twenty-three layers of ancient sites.
4. Harappa in Pakistan was 350 km away from Rakhigarhi in Haryana and 650 km from Mohenjo-daro in Pakistan.
5. Before being shipped, Harappan packages, to prevent tampering, were covered with cloth, tied down with thick twine and then sealed with soft clay sporting impressions of animals – often the unicorn/bull – which hardened.
6. In Roopkund, 16,000 feet above sea level, at the bottom of a small valley, is a frozen lake full of

human skeletons going back to 850 CE. Could a brutal hailstorm have killed them?

7. The sixteenth-century missionary Antonio Andrade reportedly went in search of, and found, an isolated wealthy kingdom in Tibet – encountering what he thought was a Christian community – that was similar to the fictional Shangri-La.
8. In 2021, archaeologists in Saudi Arabia discovered a 2,550-year-old carving of the last king of Babylon, Nabonidus, holding a sceptre.
9. Roadside vats discovered in ancient Rome collected human urine to wash and launder clothes.
10. Advanced tools, more than 2,00,000 years old, found in Africa have been found in Attirampakkam in south India too.
11. Archaeologists digging a well in China found as many as 8,000 clay terracotta soldier-statues and full-sized terracotta horses and chariots too, in a mausoleum of the first emperor of China, Qin Shi Huang.
12. Hierakonpolis, a 5,000-year-old town along the Nile River, when excavated, was found to have the remains of elephants, several baboons and a hippo, raised as pets.
13. The oldest analogue computer is the unearthed Antikythera mechanism built by Greek scientists between 205 to 80 BCE.
14. Three mythical cities that turned into reality: Nineveh in Iraq, rediscovered in the nineteenth

century; Vinland, a Viking kingdom whose relics were discovered in Canada in 1960; and Hattusa of the Hittite Empire in Turkey in the twentieth century.

15. The world's oldest artefacts found so far are 3.3-million-year-old handmade stone anvils, cores and flakes unearthed at the Lomekwi 3 site, West Turkana in Kenya.
16. The oldest known human bone is a jawbone dating back 2.8 million years found in Ethiopia along with the 'Omo one' (*Homo sapiens*) bones some 2,33,000 years old.
17. Varanasi, also known as Kashi or Benares, 5,000 years old, is the oldest city in India.
18. One of the most famous artefact in the world – the Rosetta Stone – is an ancient slab with a carved royal Ptolemaic decree dated 196 BCE; it was found in Egypt.
19. The famous Dead Sea Scrolls, 2,600 years old – 250 BCE to 68 CE – found by a shepherd in 1940 inside a ceramic jar in a cave near the Dead Sea in Qumran were found to be copies of Genesis, Exodus, Isaiah, Kings and Deuteronomy, as well as hymns, calendars and psalms and the earliest known parts of the Hebrew Bible.
20. The earliest known – until recently – human ancestor of the species Australopithecus afarensis (apes) – two-legged 'Lucy', a 3.18-million-year-old female hominid (ape) skeleton, and named after the Beatles song 'Lucy in the sky with diamonds', was found in 1974 in the Afar Triangle region of Hadar, Ethiopia by palaeontologists, Donald Johanson and Thomas Gray.

SELECT BIBLIOGRAPHY

1. Nayanjot Lahiri: *Finding Forgotten Cities,* Permanent Black in association with Ashoka University, 2005.
2. Hiram Bingham: *Lost City of the Incas,* Weidenfeld & Nicolson, 2011.
3. Raghavan Srinivasan: *Indian Cities,* Hachette India, 2023.
4. David Grann: *The Lost City of Z,* Simon & Schuster, 2010.
5. Srinivas & J. Prabhakar: *Mahabalipuram,* Thangathamarai Patthippagam, 2022.
6. Robert Sewell: *A Forgotten Empire: Vijayanagar,* General Press, 2023.
7. Philip Matyszak: *Lost Cities of the Ancient World,* Thames & Hudson, 2023.
8. Chandra S. Prasad: *Nalanda its Mahavira and Xuan Zang,* Eastern Book Linkers, 2016.
9. Namit Arora: *Indians,* Penguin Random House, 2021.
10. A. H. Longhurst: *Hampi Ruins,* Vasan Publications, 2019.
11. Joel Levy: *Lost Cities of the Ancient World,* New Holland Publishers, 2011.
12. S. R. Rao: *The Lost City of Dvaraka,* Aditya Prakashan, 2018.
13. Shah Rukh: *Mysteries of the Lost Cities,* n.p., 2024.

ACKNOWLEDGEMENTS

You, my young friends, thank you for making the effort to accompany me on this journey through the lost cities of the world. I hope you've enjoyed the excitement of finding them and the thrill of uncovering their mysteries. Thank you, Vatsala Kaul Banerjee, editor par excellence, for making this delightful journey possible. And thank you to the wonderfully meticulous Sanya Verma and the Hachette India team for giving *In Search of Lost Cities* this much-needed airing.

IMAGE COPYRIGHT INFORMATION

THE AMERICAS

Page 12: Colonel Percy Harrison Fawcett (1911), Wikimedia Commons Public Domain, Source: User Daniel Candido on pt. wikipedia; **Page 13:** Page 1 of Manuscript 512 (1753), Wikimedia Commons PD; **Page 18:** Welsh buccaneer Henry Morgan (1681), Wikimedia Commons PD, Author: Alexandre Exquemelin, Blackbeard the Pirate (1736), Wikimedia Commons PD, Author: Joseph Nicholls/ James Basire; **Page 20:** Portrait of a Man, Said to be Christopher Columbus, CC0 1.0 Universal Public Domain Dedication, Artist: Sebastiano del Piombo; **Page 24:** Muisca raft, CCA-SA 2.0 Generic license, Author: Pedro Szekely; **Page 25:** Francisco de Orellana, CCA-SA 4.0 International license, Author: Dominio publico; **Page 26:** Sir Walter Raleigh (1598), Wikimedia Commons PD, Artist: Attributed to Sir William Segar; **Page 30:** Intihuatana (solar clock) at Machu Picchu, CCA-SA 2.0 Generic license, Author: Jordan Klein; **Page 33:** Pizarro Seizing the Inca of Peru, Wikimedia Commons PD, Artist: Millais, John Everett (Sir); **Page 35:** Hiram Bingham (1917), Wikimedia Commons PD, Author: Harris & Ewing, photographer; **Page 40:** The Lost Colony, originally posted to **Flickr** by Internet Archive Book Images at https://flickr.com/photos/126377022@

N07/14781233224, Design by William Ludwell Sheppard, Engraving by William James Linton.

ASIA

Page 54: A painting of Dwarka, Wikimedia Commons PD, Author: Grindlay's; **Page 58:** Johann Ludwig Burckhardt, Wikimedia Commons PD; **Page 59:** Theatre in Petra, CCA-SA 2.0 Generic license, Author: Douglas Perkins; **Page 74:** Vittala temple, CCA-SA 4.0 International license, Author: Harshap3001; **Page 84:** Bronze replica of King Jayavarman VII, CCA-SA 3.0 Unported license, Attribution: Walters Art Museum; **Page 93:** Alexander Cunningham, Wikimedia Commons PD; **Page 102:** Mosaic of Marco Polo (1867), Wikimedia Commons PD, Author: Salviati; **Page 108:** Dhanushkodi, CCA-SA 4.0 International license, Author: D Kartikeyan; **Page 111:** Ramayana painting, Wikimedia Commons PD; **Page 117:** Division of Buddha Relics, CCA-SA 3.0 Unported license, Author: Biswarup Ganguly; **Page 130:** Dharmarajika stupa, CCA-SA 3.0 Unported license, Author: Sasha Isachenko; **Page 142:** Harappan small figures, CCA-SA 2.0 Generic license, was originally posted to **Flickr** by Trish Mayo at https://www.flickr.com/photos/97402095@N00/3304010414, Trish Mayo; **Page 151:** The Priest-King, CCA-SA 1.0 Generic license, Author: Mamoon Mengal, The Dancing Girl: Wikimedia Commons PD, Author: Alfred Nawrath; **Page 152:** Pashupati Seal: Wikimedia Commons PD; **Page 156:** Signboard, GNU Free Documentation License, CCA-SA 3.0 Unported license, Author: Siyajkak; **Page 160:** Vijaya Dharma Suri with L. P. Tessitori (1923), Wikimedia

Commons PD; **Page 167:** Lothal seals, GODL, Author: ASI; **Page 175:** Skeleton, CCA-SA 3.0 Unported license, Author: Nomu420.

AFRICA/EUROPE/OCEANIA

Page 183: Egyptian God Hapi, CC0 1.0 Universal Public Domain Dedication, Author: PharaohCrab; **Page 196:** The Last Day of Pompeii, Wikimedia Commons PD, Artist: Karl Bryullov; **Page 212:** Achilles and Patroclus, Wikimedia Commons PD; **Page 215:** Heinrich Schliemann (1878), Wikimedia Commons PD; **Page 222:** Map of the Atlantean Empire (1822), Wikimedia Commons PD, Author: Ignatius Donnelly; **Page 229:** Painting of James Cook, Wikimedia Commons PD, Author: E. Phillips Fox.